THE ROAD TO

SOMEWHERE

THE ROAD TO
SOMEWHERE

A GUIDE FOR YOUNG MEN AND WOMEN

CARLOS E. ASAY

BOOKCRAFT

Salt Lake City, Utah

Library of Congress Catalog Card Number: 94-79268
ISBN 0-88494-956-7

First Printing, 1994

Printed in the United States of America

Contents

     Obey the Eternal Rhythm of Life   *94*

PART III   *Pay Close Attention to the Road Signs Posted*   *101*

7   A Word of Caution to Young Women:
     Lust Is Not Love   *105*

8   A Charge to Young Men:
     Keep Right—Be Men of God   *113*

9   An Invitation to Young Men and Women:
     Yield to the Enticings of the Holy Spirit   *120*

     Conclusion: Youth of the Noble Birthright   *133*

     Epilogue: Would You Sell?   *138*

     Index   *143*

Preface

I have often shared with young men and women and leaders of youth the "centerpiece" experience reported in detail in the Prologue of this book. This personal experience, in company with related counsel, has caused many listeners to ask, "Why don't you write a book and share your advice with a broader audience?" Though some may have asked the question with tongue in cheek or simply to be polite, I have responded with this publication.

I have also felt an inner urge to provide my grandchildren with printed counsel about growing up and making the most of one's opportunities in life. While one or two might remember and profit from something I have said in informal family gatherings, surely more than that will refer to my words and heed suggestions given in the permanent record of a book. And after all, each generation has some responsibility for the next. Said President Spencer W. Kimball, "Whether we recognize it or not, we are connected with our past, and we can fashion a better future if we draw upon the inspiration of the past and the lessons of history, both as a people and individually" (1980 World Conference on Records).

Many people have assisted with this project and provided encouragement along the way. I acknowledge the ongoing inspiration received from my wife, Colleen. She continues to be my inspiration, my most loyal supporter, and my "beloved colleague."

I also acknowledge with appreciation the professional assistance of my secretary, Margie McKnight, and of Cory Maxwell and George Bickerstaff. All three have extended me valuable suggestions and ideas.

I am indebted to several friends who read the early drafts of this material and offered constructive criticism. Many of the suggested changes were accepted, and all of them were appreciated.

Most of the stories included in the book are accounts of actual happenings. Names have been changed in most cases to preserve the anonymity of persons involved.

This book is not an official publication of The Church of Jesus Christ of Latter-day Saints. I alone am responsible for the views it expresses.

Prologue
A Beet Field Lesson

*E*arly one Saturday morning, my father came to my bedroom and asked if I would be willing to work that day on the Church welfare farm. The assignment was to thin beets in the company of other volunteer laborers from our rural community. Though I had other things planned for that day, I agreed to help, providing the job would be completed by noon.

I was an expert at this slave-like labor—a labor that required a person to walk in a stooped position up and down rows of sugar beets, chopping with a small hoe in one hand and pulling excess plants with the other. It was a tedious task requiring more brawn than brain and more endurance than expertise. However, I could do nearly an acre in one day if I started before sun-up, ended long after sundown, and cared little about the pain of standing erect afterwards.

One of the older workers at the farm on that occasion was my stake president, a banker by profession. He was a businessman not accustomed to manual labor. In all honesty, it pleased me to see him digging in the soil and sweating under the hot sun, for this was the first time I had seen this very proper and fastidious Church leader dressed in anything other

1

than a dark suit, white shirt, and conservative tie. And I must admit that I enjoyed watching him get dirt on his hands and clothes. (I was so carried away by this pleasure [heaven forgive me!] that I sped up the soiling process by deliberately kicking up clouds of dust in his direction whenever I worked by his side.)

When the task was nearly completed, President H. Roland Tietjen invited me to speak with him. I stopped my work, laid down my hoe, and sat upon the soft ground beside the kindly man who was one of the most respected citizens in the town.

He asked, "Carlos, how old are you?"

"Eighteen," I replied.

"Do you know how old I am?" he continued.

"Oh, about seventy," was my quick and foolish answer. (I missed the mark by several years.)

Laughing without and, I supposed, crying within, he said, "My time on earth is running out; yours is just beginning. Carlos, would you sell to me the next ten years of your life?"

I thought to myself, What is wrong with President Tietjen? Can't he forget buying and selling for just one morning?

He was able to discern my thoughts and to sense my discomfort with the improbable proposition placed before me. Said he: "I know it is impossible for you to transfer part of your life to me. But if it were possible, would you sell?"

"No!" I blurted out with little thought or reflection. "I would not sell to you or anyone else."

"Suppose I offered you a hundred thousand dollars for these ten years," he pressed. (This was before the day of double- and triple-digit inflation.)

Again I declined his offer, asserting that I had things to do in the years ahead and that I would not sell a part of my life for any amount of money.

During the ten years that followed the beet field conversation, my visits with President Tietjen were few and scattered. Yet, whenever we met, he would refer back to the original question and ask, "Will you accept ninety thousand dollars for the remaining nine years? Eighty thousand for the next eight?" And so it went until the ten years had come and gone.

It did not require a full decade for me to appreciate the profound lesson my wonderful and caring Church leader had taught. I knew he loved me and wanted me to make the most of my life. I knew he wanted me to treasure those formative years between eighteen and twenty-eight—a time when important decisions of eternal consequence are made. Moreover, I knew he wanted to motivate me to set goals, make plans, and initiate actions that would enable me to make the most of my future opportunities.

Would You Sell?

Whenever I meet with young men and women, I think about President Tietjen and the lesson he taught me years ago while working in a beet field. I find myself wondering what price or value teenagers place upon the next ten years of their lives. I wonder whether they would be willing to exchange a decade of living for money or things that money can buy.

All of us know it is impossible for someone to package a portion of his or her life and peddle it to another. It is possible, however, for the young to squander the prospects of the immediate future by allowing time to slip away without developing talents, grasping opportunities, or building toward a desirable end.

An ancient prophet gave this timeless advice: "Do not spend money for that which is of no worth, nor your labor for that which cannot satisfy."[1] Though this warning is applicable to men and women of all ages, it seems to hold special meaning for the young. I say this because pursuit of the quick and easy things causes many young people to lose sight of all the better things that money cannot buy.

The squanderer is one who wastes time, who allows talents to remain hidden, opportunities to slip away, and worthy goals to float in limbo. He is like the thief who picks his own pocket or the fool who beats his head against the brick wall. Squanderers are easily satisfied and easily lulled away into carnal security by negative influences, so that they say: "All is well . . . all is well—and thus the devil cheateth their souls, and leadeth them away carefully down to hell."[2] So, too, will it be for youth who allow the impressionable years to come and go like a dream in the night without choosing desired destinations and without charting proper courses.

Major Decisions

Many crucial decisions are made by young men and women in the late teen years and the early twenties, such as: What career path shall I follow? Shall I pursue a profession or become involved in some vocational work? Shall I seek advanced learning at a university or attend a vocational school? Shall I serve a full-time mission for the Church? With whom shall I associate? Who will I marry? Will it be a marriage for time only or a marriage for both time and for all eternity? Where will I live? What kind of a parent will I be? The answers to these and similar questions will have bearing upon one's lifestyle, one's standard of living, and other aspects of life. In fact, the what, why, where, when, and how of living for the rest of one's experience on earth are largely determined in the decade of eighteen to twenty-eight. Hence these precious years must not be approached without serious forethought.

In the Broadway musical *Fiddler on the Roof*, Tevye sings:

> Sunrise, sunset,
> Swiftly fly the years,
> One season following another,
> Laden with happiness and tears.[3]

The years do come and go in rapid succession, especially as one grows older. And they truly are filled with happiness and tears. I am convinced, however, that the seasons of happiness will far outnumber the seasons of tears for those who make the right decisions during the critical years of youth and anticipate the future with faith and a worthy plan of action.

Birthrights

Esau, the eldest son of Isaac, was "a cunning hunter, a man of the field," a young man who was entitled to a special birthright, according to the Old Testament record. One day Esau returned home from the field hungry and weary after a day's work—perhaps heavy labor in hot and oppressive weather. Said he to his brother, Jacob, "Feed me, I pray thee, with that same red pottage; for I am faint." Jacob responded: "Sell me this day thy birthright." "I am at the point to die," said Esau, "and what profit shall this birthright do to me?" So "Jacob gave Esau bread and pottage of lentiles; and he did eat and drink, and rose up, and went his way." The account closes with the sad words, "Thus Esau despised his birthright."[4]

Some young people, like Esau of old, despise their birthright and sell it for a "morsel of meat"[5] or a momentary thrill. Their minds and hearts seem fixed upon the here and now. They seem unwilling to pay the price of something greater than that which fills the stomach or satisfies a lust. In the end, they come to the painful realization that their right to a fulness of living and a fulness of joy has been forfeited.

My plea and my challenge to all young people is cradled in two related questions: Would you sell the next ten years of your life for X dollars? Are you doing whatever is necessary to avoid squandering all the future holds for you?

Keep in mind these inspired lines:

> Time flies on wings of lightning;
> We cannot call it back.
> It comes, then passes forward
> Along its onward track.
> And if we are not mindful,
> The chance will fade away,
> For life is quick in passing,
> 'Tis as a single day.[6]

Yes, the next ten years of your life will come and go just as surely as the sun rises and sets each day. Now is the time to catch a bright vision of your future and set it deep in your mind and heart. Today is the time to build for a tomorrow free of regret and full of wonderful blessings.

You must decide now not to squander your great privileges, never to sell your noble birthright.

Notes

1. 2 Nephi 9:51.
2. 2 Nephi 28:21.
3. *Fiddler on the Roof*, 1964.
4. See Genesis 25:22–34.
5. See Hebrews 12:16–17.
6. "Improve the Shining Moments," *Hymns*, no. 226.

Introduction
Highwaymen Along the Slippery Path of Youth

*B*efore the day of the automobile, travel was done by foot, on horses, or in wagons drawn by domesticated animals. Roads were mostly narrow dirt paths, hardened by the flow of traffic. In densely populated areas the roads were well defined and safe to move upon, but in the more remote areas, where the trails twisted over hills and through the forests, the roads were dangerous and, in earlier centuries, were often infested by men on horseback who robbed travelers. Such thieves were called highwaymen.

Highwaymen were sly and devious rogues who took advantage of others. They were predators with little or no conscience, as illustrated in this excerpt from a short story:

> In a desert region one day, a number of travelers set out on a trip. . . . At the end of [a] day, two of the group, half-blinded by dust and with their strength nearly gone, came unexpectedly, with something more than good fortune, upon an inn and way station. There in the sanctuary of

walls and roof, they refreshed themselves and counted their blessings. There they replenished their stores and contemplated the remaining portion of their journey. The weather remained unsettled. The wind continued to blow. The poorly marked road wound ahead through hills where the sand piled deep and where it was said that robbers sometimes preyed upon unsuspecting travelers.

One of the two was anxious to reach his destination. He had important business in the city. He gathered his supplies and water and paid his account. Early in the morning he set out in haste in an attempt to cross the hill country by nightfall. But the windblown sand had blocked the road. He was forced to dig and detour. When night came, he was far from the city, exhausted and alone. When he fell asleep, thieves [highwaymen] found him, took his supplies, and left him without strength and without water to face almost certain death.[1]

There are two highwaymen or thugs who stalk the young and steal their supplies and sap their strength as they travel the slippery path of youth. (I use the expression "slippery" because it is so easy to slip or slide and even fall during this critical time of life.) One of the thugs is called Blindness of Mind and the other is known as Hardness of Heart. Both are sinister influences; both have satanic origins; and both have the same objective, which is to mislead, rob, and, if possible, destroy the rising generation.

Blindness of Mind

Blindness of Mind, like the thieves in the account above, preys upon the unsuspecting. He picks the pockets of youth by (1) stifling their desire to set *goals,* (2) stifling their desire to develop personal *gifts and talents,* and (3) drawing their minds and eyes away from *worthy role models.* Thus he leaves his victims wandering aimlessly over the countryside without a purpose or compass to provide them with direction.

Blindness of Mind is, indeed, a shadowy character who

knows that if he can pull a veil over the eyes and minds of young people, thus obscuring their view of desirable destinations, they will give up or quit before reaching the end. He therefore whispers into the ears of would-be listeners that goal setting and planning ahead are childish behaviors and are not worth doing. "After all," he says, "it doesn't matter which road you take or whether you ever arrive at some predetermined place." He adds, "Don't get uptight; just flow along with the crowd and have fun along the way."

Another tactic of Blindness of Mind is to convince the impressionable young that they are ill equipped to accomplish much of significance in life. In subtle and devious ways he plants seeds of doubt in the minds of listeners and tries to convince them that their personal gifts are very limited and that any attempts to develop talents will be too difficult, too drawn out, too painful, and totally unnecessary. His deadly talk includes statements such as: "You are no good;" "You can't do it;" "You have nothing special or unique to contribute;" and "Even if you did have a flair for something, it wouldn't be worthwhile for you or anyone else to pursue it." Yes, Blindness of Mind would have you believe that mediocrity is a crown-jewel virtue and that being a spectator is safer than and preferable to being an active player in the game of life.

Moreover, Blindness of Mind would have youth scoff at the idea of selecting heroes or heroines and following in the footsteps of worthy role models. Says he: "Do your own thing! Don't become hemmed in by the manner in which another person lives, especially if that person is older and of the past." All role models, according to Blindness of Mind, are old-fashioned, have clay feet, and are full of hypocrisy. Hence, he claims, they cannot be trusted and certainly should not be emulated.

Whenever a young person loses his way or falls short of the mark, no one laughs louder than Blindness of Mind. He glories in wasted lives, particularly when that waste is caused by a fuzzy view of what might have been.

Blindness of mind is really spiritual darkness. It is a condition or state of mind that alienates people, young or old, from godly matters. Those who suffer from this awful condition fail to see the hand of providence manifest in the affairs of mankind. They believe only in that which can be seen and felt and hefted. In effect, a dark curtain of unbelief has been drawn over their minds, causing them to see little or no purpose in their being.

Much like the sightless man who cautiously makes his way down the street tapping his cane to identify the hazards that lie ahead, the person "blind of mind" stumbles awkwardly through life. Every step is tentative; each roadblock is almost insurmountable; and progress is painfully slow at best. Of such people it is said they "have eyes to see, and see not"; "Their eyes cannot see afar off"; they "shall see, and shall not perceive."[2]

Hardness of Heart

Hardness of Heart, an accomplice of Blindness of Mind, strips youth of such valuables as (1) a willingness to obey God's commandments, (2) a willingness to accept parental guidance, and (3) a willingness to live in accord with the laws of nature. He rejoices over his victims who are left only with a rebellious spirit and with their heritage hanging in jeopardy.

Whenever the expression "blindness of mind" is used in the scriptures, it is almost always accompanied by the words "hardness of heart." This is not surprising to those who understand the workings of the Spirit and who know what happens to people who fail to "look to God and live."[3] Those who lose their vision of sacred matters inevitably become unfeeling, calloused, and unsympathetic toward religion and all that it encompasses. One writer summarized: "The eyes of the people were blinded; *therefore* they hardened their hearts against the words of [God]."[4]

Hardness of Heart is a cold and calculating monster with one object in mind—to cause young people to openly rebel against heaven and home. He would have all young men and women waste their inheritances, eat with swine, and become prodigal sons and daughters.[5] Hardness of Heart considers law, especially divine law, as something unnecessarily confining. So he argues, "Don't become a slave to some unknown being, for no man can know of things which cannot be seen." Moreover, he states, "every man prospers in this life according to his own genius and strength; therefore, whatsoever a man does is no crime."[6] With such dishonest talk, Hardness of Heart leads youth "by the neck with a flaxen cord, until he [binds] them with his strong cords forever."[7]

But Hardness of Heart is not content with simply turning people away from God. He would have his followers reject all forms of authority, including parental authority. He refers to parental instructions as the foolish traditions of fathers and mothers. "Cut the apron strings" is his oft-repeated line. "Be your own man; show your independence; and live for the here-and-now." Through these and other fallacious arguments the tender and chaste hearts of youth are turned to stone and the blessings associated with honoring parents are lost forever.

One more damning influence related to Hardness of Heart should be mentioned. I speak of the temptation placed before youth to disobey laws of nature, to ignore the proper preparation for each new experience, and to force the sequence in which life's experiences should come. There are seductive voices that ask young people: "What is wrong with dating in your early teens?" "Why wait for marriage to have sexual experience?" "Why not have a baby now?" "Why not jump into the adult world as soon as possible?" These voices persuade many to face grown-up responsibilities well before they have grown up; and having forsaken the eternal scheme of things (God's planned order of events), they find they have passed over many of life's greatest experiences and enjoyments and are left with lifetime regrets.

You need to realize that hardness of heart is a gradual, subtle illness and not a massive heart attack that comes with little or no warning. It begins with the breaking of a single law. It grows layer by layer as more and more commandments are flaunted and as one thus becomes less and less able to distinguish between right and wrong. Then, as time lapses and rebellion increases, the once gentle and feeling heart becomes an impenetrable flint. No one is more hardened in character than he who has, without repenting, transgressed the laws of God, the laws of loving parents, and the laws of nature.

Road Signs and Faces

Hardness of Heart and Blindness of Mind are not individuals with physical bodies of flesh and bones who can be seen with the eye or touched by a hand. They are, however, just as real as the air we breathe. The reflection of one is seen in the faces of law-breakers; the image of the other is seen in the faces of those without hope or faith in the future. Both mirror unhappiness and indicate that the person has chosen to listen to an evil spirit.[8]

I have never seen either Hardness of Heart or Blindness of Mind, or the evil one who sired them. I know that they exist, however, because I have observed the results of their influence. I see them smiling each time a young person confuses lust with love and suffers the loss of virtue. I see them sneering each time a young person makes the wrong turn and fails to become what he or she ought to become. And I hear them laugh out loud[9] each time a young person listens to their temptings and receives the wages of sin.

On the other hand, I have seen evidences of Satan and his highwaymen disappear when people have stayed on the right path and observed carefully the posted road signs. Satan's influences cannot abide light and truth. They flee from light and truth just as the darkness of the night flees in the presence of the rays of the morning sun. Shadows cast by Hardness of Heart and Blindness of Mind are chased away by those who possess true love, who have the honest desire to become men and women of God, and who have willingly accepted the invitation to yield to the enticings of the Holy Spirit.

An ancient prophet asked this piercing question: "Can ye look up to God . . . with a pure heart and clean hands? . . . Can you look up, having the image of God engraven upon your countenances?"[10] Faces do mirror the inner soul. Those who make mistakes suffer embarrassment—"Their faces shall be as flames";[11] those who sin are promised "the [show] of their countenance doth witness against them";[12] but those who exercise faith and engage in good works reflect godly influences and have faces that will "shine exceedingly, even as the faces of angels."[13]

Exceeding Faith and Good Works

We read of some individuals who were "called and pre-pared from the foundation of the world according to the fore-knowledge of God, on account of their exceeding faith and good works." The same scripture makes reference also to others who rejected "the Spirit of God on account of the hardness of their hearts and blindness of their minds, while, if it had not been for this they might have had as great privilege as their brethren."[14]

We must not conclude from the scripture cited above that we came to earth with our future predetermined. This is not the case. We enjoy moral agency in this life, and hence, through the principle of repentance, we can always improve and do better (or by ignoring that principle we can do worse). But some very important conclusions may be drawn from the scriptural verses just cited, along with other sacred teachings. For example: (1) people who exercise "exceeding faith" and who show forth "good works" receive greater privileges than those who don't; (2) people who are unbelieving and who rebel against God and all righteousness become hard of heart and blind of mind be-cause they drive the Spirit of God from their presence; and (3) people who have "an eye of faith" and who have "the law written in their hearts" will not only enjoy the companionship of the Holy Spirit but also will receive special blessings and promises.[15]

It is said that hope mounts high in youth. Such seems to be the case because most young people look forward, not back-ward, as some older folks do. Moreover, they harbor all kinds of dreams for the future, expecting that the years ahead will bring a flood of blessings. So it is essential that members of the rising generation remember this simple yet eternal truth: Just as two parts of hydrogen and one part of oxygen form water, so do the elements of "exceeding faith," "good works," and "attention to the road signs posted along the path of youth" constitute the means of success and happiness in the lives of young men and women. Expressed in formula form, this eternal truth—a truth that constitutes the thesis of this book—is shown in the accom-panying illustration.

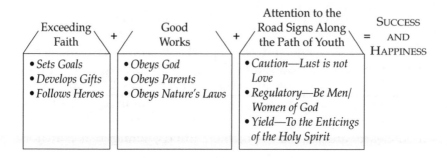

Those who exercise "exceeding faith" will set goals, recognize and develop personal gifts, and follow worthy role models. Those who participate in "good works" will obey God, obey parents, and obey the eternal rhythm of life. (Faith and good works invite the Spirit of God into one's life so that synergistic powers will be received.) Then, when youth heed the caution, regulatory, and yield signs posted along the slippery path of youth, success and happiness will be the inevitable result.

Every individual who walks through life will at one time or another meet the two highwaymen or thugs discussed in this introduction. You will be no exception. It may be a head-on confrontation; or it may come subtly in an unsuspecting moment. But however quietly or traumatically the meeting occurs, you must be prepared to face the challenge by exercising *exceeding faith*, showing forth *good works*, and heeding the posted *road signs*. Such readiness and defense rallies the full spiritual powers found within you and puts to flight any would-be-intruder who seeks to rob, to plunder, or to dash your hopes for the future.

Notes

1. F. Burton Howard, *Ensign,* May 1981, pp. 71–72.
2. See Ezekiel 12:2; Moses 6:27; Matthew 13:14.
3. Alma 37:47.

4. Mosiah 11:29; emphasis added.
5. See Luke 15:11–19.
6. See Alma 30:6–60.
7. 2 Nephi 26:22.
8. See Alma 3:26–27.
9. See Moses 7:26.
10. Alma 5:19.
11. Isaiah 13:8.
12. Isaiah 3:9.
13. Helaman 5:36.
14. Alma 13:3–4.
15. See Ether 12:19; Romans 2:15.

PART I

To Avoid Blindness of Mind—
Exercise Exceeding Faith

*I*n my youth we played a parlor game called Blindman's Buff, a game in which a blindfolded player had to catch and identify another player. The game evolved as follows: First, a cloth or blindfold was placed over the eyes of one player; second, the person blindfolded was turned around and around by the other players so that he became dizzy, disoriented, and out of balance; third, the one blindfolded was then challenged to grope in the dark about the room until he caught another player; and finally, the blindman was required to identify the person within his grasp using only his senses of feel, smell, and sound. If proper identification was made, the person caught and identified became the blindman. If not, the blindman was required to try again.

I remember how helpless I felt when the cloth was placed over my eyes. And I recall how very confusing and uncomfortable it was to be spun about and placed off balance. It was truly a frustrating feeling to lose visual contact with the group and to not know where I was or where I was going.

Young people who fail to set goals, cultivate personal gifts and talents, and select righteous role models are sucked into a type of blindman's buff whether they want to be in it or not. By neglecting to define desired objectives, they tie a blindfold over their own eyes and hence see little beyond their own noses. They spin themselves around and around and lose their equilibrium when they divert their eyes from the steady role models who could serve as compass points. And they add to their self-imposed blindness of mind by doubting their own worth and capabilities. Make no mistake about it, no one who suffers from blindness of mind ever comes off the winner in blindman's buff or in any other game, particularly the game we call life.

Faith, even exceeding faith, is the only sure cure of the spiritual myopia or nearsightedness we call blindness of mind. One who exercises faith and has confidence in his or her abilities to achieve does not hesitate to pursue openly declared purposes. Nor does he or she hesitate to profit from the mistakes and successes of others. Rather, he reaches out for the steadying influence of others, reaches down into the depths of his own God-given resources, and stretches himself toward the noble ends before him. In the process of all of this, he looks at life through the "eye of faith" (Ether 12:19), pushes aside gloomy doubts, and dispels the clouds of darkness that hover over his head.

CHAPTER 1

To Avoid Blindness of Mind—
Set Worthy Goals and Strive to Reach Them

*P*resident Thomas S. Monson related this experience with a moral:

> Several days ago, while driving to my home, . . . I noticed three hitchhikers, each one of whom carried a homemade sign which announced his desired destination. One sign read "Los Angeles," while a second carried the designation "Boise." However, it was the third sign which not only caught my attention but caused me to reflect and ponder its message. The hitchhiker had lettered not Los Angeles, California, nor Boise, Idaho, on the cardboard sign which he held aloft. Rather, his sign consisted of but one word and read simply "ANYWHERE."
>
> Here was one who was content to travel in any direction, according to the whim of the driver who stopped to give him a free ride. What an enormous price to pay for such a ride. No plan. No objective. No goal. The road to anywhere is the road to nowhere, and the road to nowhere leads to dreams sacrificed, opportunities squandered, and a life unfulfilled.[1]

Tumbleweed Existence

Young people who hold aloft the sign marked Anywhere have surrendered to that thug called Blindness of Mind, and they have become pawns of time, circumstance, and every tide of influence. Since they have no destination or goal in mind, they follow the path of least resistance and flow lazily with the stream of events around them. Some are unwittingly drawn into rough waters that thrash them about mercilessly. Others wash into dangerous eddies where they move against the main current and go around and around until they get into serious trouble. Still others are pushed into still waters where they sit, grow stale, and stink. Whatever the case, those without goals in mind may be likened to the ancients of America who were found to be "even as chaff is driven before the wind, or as a vessel is tossed about upon the waves, without sail or anchor, or without anything wherewith to steer her."[2]

A modern prophet stated that those who live an unplanned and haphazard life, like the hitchhiker bound for Anywhere, are living a tumbleweed existence. He explained:

> Over the Utah plains, upon the hillsides and along the fence-lines of the valleys, grows the tumbleweed. When mature and dry, the plant breaks from its roots and, as a rounded tangle of light stiff branches, rolls about like a ball. If the wind blows west, the weed rolls against the western fences. With each direction change in the wind, the rounded weed rolls with it, following lines of least resistance until stopped by fences or walls or ditch banks. As the wind blows down the road, the tumbleweeds go rolling like mammoth marbles thrown from a giant hand.
>
> Many people, and particularly many of our youth, live a "tumbleweed" existence. They tend to follow leadership which is dominant and powerful, regardless of whether it is right or wrong.[3]

Whether a person flows lazily with the stream of events around him or, like a tumbleweed, rolls hither or thither with the prevailing winds, the results are much the same. There is no purposeful movement, no zestful living, and no meaningful progress in the lives of those who live a tumbleweed existence. On the other hand, when a person has an openly declared goal in mind he assumes control of his life and moves forward with purpose. His step is sure and his actions are calculated to bring success.

Getting to Madison Square Garden

Allow me to illustrate the importance of goals and right-eous intent by sharing with you a personal account entitled "Getting to Madison Square Garden." You too will have your dreams of reaching some goal or attaining some worthy objec-tive. It may not be getting to "the Garden," as I did, but it will involve a process of striving and growing similar to what I have experienced.

Soon after I turned fourteen years of age I was ordained a teacher in the Aaronic Priesthood and assigned as a ward teacher (what is now called a home teacher). The Melchizedek Priesthood bearer appointed as my companion was Melvin Jensen, a man several years my senior. He assumed the lead in scheduling the appointments and in conducting the discussions in the homes. However, he did involve me in the visits in such a way as to provide me with positive experiences.

One night, as we walked toward the final appointment for the evening, Mel paused with me under a streetlight and en-gaged me in conversation. Among other things, he asked me questions about my future. One specific question was, "What is your great ambition in life?"

I hesitated momentarily—not because I didn't have a goal in mind, but because I feared that my response might sound silly to him. Mel spoke some words of reassurance and won my complete trust. So I said what was in my heart: "Someday, I hope to play basketball in Madison Square Garden."

There was an awkward silence. I don't believe Brother Jensen expected the kind of answer I gave. Thank goodness, however, he didn't laugh at my honest expression. If he had, I believe my hopes and dreams would have been dealt a crushing blow. Instead, Mel placed his big hand upon my shoulder and said: "That's wonderful, Carlos. I know you can do it." He added further encouragement by commenting on my size and ability; and he promised me that if I would keep myself clean and practice consistently, someday my dream would come true.

Brother Jensen's words of confidence lifted me more than I can describe. I had shared an intimate, heartfelt desire with an adult—someone I trusted and admired—and that adult had, in turn, expressed faith in my ability to perform.

When our visits were completed that night I said goodnight to my home teaching companion and ran home. Mother was in the kitchen as I entered the house, and I wasted little time in telling her about the streetlight conversation with Mel. She too was surprised to learn about my secret ambition.

Although Mother's interest in sports was less than avid, over the years she had learned to tolerate the "game talk" and the "Monday quarterback" commentaries of her husband and four active sons, and her interest in me was genuine. She said some reassuring things and wondered just how much I knew about Madison Square Garden. I confessed that I knew very little about the place. "If the Garden is related to your goal," she commented, "why don't you become better acquainted with it?" She suggested that I might want to collect newspaper and magazine clippings of pictures and articles involving Madison Square Garden. With her help and encouragement, I did.

In the succeeding months I filled my scrapbook and became somewhat of an authority on New York City's Madison Square Garden. I recall shooting baskets by the hour at a hoop attached to an apple tree in my father's orchard, doing this in all kinds of weather. I was never alone, for the surrounding trees seemed like grandstands filled with cheering people as I lived my fantasy.

The "dream" caused me to train consistently. I tried hard to keep my body clean and to improve my abilities. I didn't want any bad habits or physical weaknesses to prevent me from reaching my goal. And as the years passed and basketball seasons came and went, I continued to pursue it.

Following high school came military and other experiences, and gradually my enthusiasm for the scrapbook ebbed. My enthusiasm for the goal itself, however, remained riveted in my mind. Whenever I practiced or played, there was always that dream of performing before thousands in Madison Square Garden. I remained pointed toward that dream.

In 1946, at the age of twenty, I enrolled at the University of Utah. That fall, as a freshman, I tried out for and won a place on the varsity basketball team. At Christmastime we toured in the eastern part of the United States. Part of our tour included a game in Madison Square Garden.

Entering the Garden the first time was almost like returning home. I had read about the place, I had seen pictures of the place, and in my mind and heart I had been there many times.

Later that same basketball season, in March 1947, I returned to Madison Square Garden with the University of Utah team to participate in the National Invitation Tournament (NIT). Thanks to a strong starting lineup consisting of Arnie Ferrin, Vern Gardner, Wat Misaka, Fred Weidner, and Leon Watson, we won the tournament. Immediately following our victory—on the playing floor of Madison Square Garden—my teammates and I were presented with beautiful Bulova wristwatches.[4]

After all these years, my Madison Square Garden watch is still being worn and it is still running! Each time I look at it I'm reminded of all the wonderful things that can happen in the life of a young man or woman of faith and good works. No one can tell me that goals are not important in the lives of youth. My watch contradicts such a claim.

Of all the truths spoken, few are more important to youth than this, "When a person does not know which harbour he or she is making for, none is the right one."

Why Goals

Have you ever thought what might happen to the game of football if you removed the goalposts and erased the goal line? How would you keep the score? How would you know whether you were winning or losing? How would you maintain interest among the players?

In my youth, I would refuse to play a game of basketball if

someone suggested that we play for "funzies" and not keep score. What purpose does the game serve if you don't receive credit for putting that ball through the little hoop? How can you get excited or motivated about your involvement in something if you don't count and mark successful efforts?[5]

I am not suggesting that the only pleasure one derives from a game or life itself is in reaching a defined goal. Much satisfaction can come from the spirited play between the goalposts as efforts are made to outwit and overcome worthy opponents, for it is the challenge that causes juices to flow and ideas to generate. But when all is said and done, it is the exhilarating act of crossing the goal line or scoring the basket that keeps one going and striving.

What a Goal Is

A goal is defined as a "line or place at which a race, trip, etc., is ended." It is also defined as "an object or end that one strives to attain."[6] Synonyms for the word *goal* include: ambition, aspiration, design, intent, purpose, aim, end, finish, mark, and target. Each of these expressions suggests a desired destination, a final product, a state of being, or some other result of our time and efforts.

Said one motivational speaker: "Success does not necessarily mean that we must earn a great deal of money and live in the biggest house in town. It means only that we are daily engaged in striving toward a goal that we have independently chosen and feel is worthy of us as persons. A goal, whatever it may be, is what gives meaning to our existence. It is the carrot on the stick that keeps us striving—that keeps us interested—that gives us a reason for getting out of bed in the morning."[7]

How very sad it is when young people have no goals in mind and are bound for anywhere. They have no genuine reason for getting out of bed in the morning. Thus they are content to live a "tumbleweed" existence.

The Ultimate Goal

Anyone who embraces the gospel of Jesus Christ, be he young or old, assumes a vested interest in God's avowed purpose or goal. This goal is stated succinctly in a verse of scripture: "This is my work and my glory—to bring to pass the immortality and eternal life of man."[8] Immortality is an accomplished fact; it is a gift of God provided to everyone through the grace and resurrection of Christ. Eternal life, however, is the big concern of our moment in mortality. So all of us should be deeply committed to two related tasks: (1) attaining eternal life (life with God and with the quality of life he enjoys) for ourselves, and (2) helping our Father in Heaven achieve his stated purpose by encouraging others to repent and come unto Christ.

No goal, no objective, no purpose, no intent, no target, no mark, and no aspiration matches in importance the ultimate goal of eternal life. Consequently that goal should appear at the top of every list made by accountable children of God. You must not allow it to be obscured by blindness of mind or any other enemy of righteousness.

In your quest for the ultimate goal, you should be guided by this God-given charge: "Ye are therefore commanded to be perfect, even as your Father who is in heaven is perfect."[9] It is unlikely that you will reach perfection while living on earth. Not all of the rough edges in your character and personality will be chiseled away by the time you die. Nonetheless, the goal of becoming complete, finished, and fully developed in whatever ways possible must not be allowed to sink out of sight. I say this because our quest for perfection is related directly to our quest for eternal life.

Enabling Goals

If you were traveling from New York to Perth, Australia, you would probably travel that long distance in four stages. One flight would take you to Los Angeles, another would move you to Honolulu, the third would carry you to Sydney, and the fourth leg of the journey would end in Perth. Perth would be your final or ultimate goal, yet each stop along the way would serve as an intermediate or short-range or enabling objective.

Those who want to attain God's greatest gift—the gift of eternal life—will not do it in one fell swoop or by taking one giant step. There are points along the way that must be touched, such as living righteously, sharing priesthood power, participating in celestial or temple marriage, and performing Christian service. Each of these points is enabling in nature and constitutes a stepping-stone on the path leading upward to eternal life—the ultimate goal.

"If we are to achieve long-range goals," advised President Ezra Taft Benson, "we must learn to set up and accomplish short-range goals that will move us along the way. If we do not consciously select our goals, we may be controlled by goals not of our own choosing—goals imposed by outside pressures (such as the expectations of others) or by our habits (such as procrastination) or by our desire for the approval of the world."[10]

Perhaps now you can understand why Church leaders plead with youth to seek an education, receive the temple endowment, serve a mission, marry in the temple, master useful work skills, raise families, and achieve other enabling objectives of a refining and perfecting nature.

Basic Principles of Setting Goals

Not all people define goals in the same words or approach goal setting in the same manner. For instance, those involved in selling cars address the subject rather differently than those who instruct in a classroom. The one group deals with the exchange of tangible goods; the other is involved in the imparting of knowledge and the development of intangible qualities. Moreover, the athlete on the track may not use goals in the same way or as precisely as a scientist in a laboratory would. Yet there are some basic principles of goal setting that seem to be commonly accepted by most experts and applied to all, whether in the laboratory, the track, the classroom, or the sales office. They are as follows:

Goals should be personal, not imposed by others. Imposed goals are impersonal and become quotas in most people's minds. They can, therefore, become very burdensome, unrealistic, and quite objectionable. On the other hand, goals that are self-made and self-imposed draw a commitment born of strong desire. Few perform well under forced conditions, especially if those conditions run counter to one's innermost feelings. But when one performs willfully and according to internalized standards, good things happen. So take the initiative and set your own goals—build high expectations for yourself.

Goals should be challenging, yet attainable. Some people contend that goals should be of the "pie-in-the-sky" variety and always set beyond one's reach. I disagree with this point of view because it tends to condition people to failure.

If a young man is participating in the high-jumping event and the bar is always placed just a little higher than the limits of his ability, he will lose interest in the sport after so many failed attempts. But when the bar is set at a challenging yet attainable level, and he succeeds in clearing it, he will ask that it be raised so that another level may be tried. It is the thrill of clearing the bar—attaining the goal—that keeps him striving and pushing toward greater heights.

President Spencer W. Kimball is often quoted as saying: "Goals should always be made to a point that will make us reach and strain. Success should not necessarily be gauged by our always reaching the goal set, but by our progress and attainment."[11] This statement, however, took on added meaning when he mentioned the motivating nature of "goals that are realistic and can be reached but always greater than before."[12]

So set goals that are challenging yet attainable, and move forward, ever reaching and straining upward.

Goals should be specific and clearly understood. A fuzzy view of a desired destination is not very inspirational to the traveler; nor does it stir his imagination. In fact, the vagueness of the objective may dampen enthusiasm and cause one to move forward slowly with a tentative step. Anyone who has stumbled in the dark, having limited light to guide him, knows what I am talking about. But when the goal or objective is clearly in mind and is stated in specific terms, a person is supplied a focal point toward which he may work with all his might. The "clear-cut" ideal and clearly defined goal becomes the star to steer by. If it is constant and focused enough it will allow us to mark progress and to check timetables.

In defining your goals, then, be as precise as the nature of your desired objectives permits. Allow the "clear-cut" ideal to guide you toward worthwhile ends.

My goal of playing basketball in Madison Square Garden was *my goal* and not something imposed upon me by others. It was challenging and attainable, not something that I could slide or ease into. And with my mother's help, the goal was specifically and clearly established in my mind's eye and planted deeply as a heartfelt desire.

A Goal-Setting Process

The last word has not been spoken or written in describing *the* process of setting goals. Only you can determine what is best for you and your circumstances. You should, however, pray, seek counsel, experiment on your own, and develop a workable procedure that expedites your efforts, not one that becomes an end in and of itself. In doing so, you may wish to include these seven steps:

Step 1: *Obtain a vision of where you want to go, of what you want to do, and of what you want to become—then set goals.* It is written: "Where there is no vision, the people perish."[13] Individualizing this statement, we might say, "Where there is no vision, a person makes little or no progress." Nephi excelled in his calling because he was faithful and his views were glorious.[14] Such will be the lot of all young people who look ahead, pray for guidance, meditate over expectations, and seek a vision of what can and ought to occur in their lives.

Have you ever taken the time to sit alone in some secluded spot and ponder your future? Have you attempted to look ahead and determine what it is that you want to do and to become? If not, do it now. Become a visionary man or woman in terms of the things that affect your future and well-being.

Step 2: *Obtain confirmation of the Spirit.* Once the vision is obtained and goals are defined, you should seek a confirmation of your intent from a higher source—a source that is made available to us through study, fasting, and prayer. Once the goal setter hears the whisperings within the chambers of his mind and heart, receives the burning in his bosom, and obtains a peace of mind relative to his intents, he will receive assurance that something is right and in accord with the divine will.[15] Such whisperings, burning, peace, and assurance could be as simple as a gentle feeling within that something is right and worth doing.

Few things are more calming to the soul than the feeling that what you are contemplating or doing is approved of the Lord.

Step 3: *Verbalize your goals for commitment purposes.* I suspect there are some goals that are too personal to be shared with anyone except the Lord. Under normal circumstances, however, it is a good practice to share your intent with someone who can provide you with ongoing encouragement, support, and applause. It may be a friend, a parent, a leader, or someone else who can be trusted and who will respect your confidence.

Verbalization of intent will serve to commit you even more to the goal and build an expectancy of performance that is highly motivating. It will also draw someone into your striving process who will monitor your progress and "keep your feet to the fire." Remember that the verbalization of goals enables you to confirm planned actions with a sympathetic supporter and places you in a position in which you might receive needed inspiration from that interested party if resolve begins to weaken.

Step 4: *Prepare a plan of action.* Said Ward Cantrell: "Apathy can be overcome by enthusiasm, and enthusiasm can be aroused by only two things: (1) an ideal (or purpose) that takes the imagination by storm; (2) a definite, intelligible plan for carrying that ideal into practice."[16]

Goals that are challenging and yet attainable do excite the imagination. Then, when a plan is drafted for achieving those goals, strong anticipation is generated. The goals and the plan work together synergistically in drawing performance upward.

Goals without plans are only dreams. Goals with plans are much more likely to become realities.

In preparing a plan of action, you must draw upon all of the creative genius within you and upon all of the spiritual gifts available.[17]

A thing must be created spiritually before it can be created temporally;[18] that is, one must picture the goal within the mind's eye and preview mentally the process of achieving the goal. You do this by anticipating all the hurdles that lie between you and your goal and by picturing yourself jumping those hurdles. You then describe the "spiritual creation" in writing, step by step, until the full plan of action is created in fact.

Step 5: *Visualize your goals for motivational purposes.* Some people write their goals on a chalkboard, or on a paper they pin to a bulletin board where they will see it every day. Others use pictures of places or persons related to their goals.

One who has in mind celestial marriage may display a picture of her favorite temple on the wall. Another who plans to serve a full-time mission may exhibit a picture of a Missionary Training Center or even a photograph of a faraway place with a strange-sounding name where his father or brother served. A picture of a college and pictures of professional workers may also be used to keep one pointed toward educational and vocational goals. And a picture of the Savior or some other worthy role model may serve as a vivid reminder of who one wants to become. Whatever the visual, if it is carefully selected and prominently displayed it will speak a thousand encouraging words in muted language to anyone who has an eye to the future and an honest longing in his or her heart.

"Genius," it is said, "is the power to visualize the objective."

Step 6: *Work diligently to reach the goals or objectives.* Note God's goal-striving determination in these scriptures:

> God doth not walk in crooked paths, neither doth he turn to the right hand nor to the left, neither doth he vary from that which he hath said, therefore his paths are straight, and his course is one eternal round.[19]

> There is nothing that the Lord thy God shall take in his heart to do but what he will do it.[20]

If these are not firm declarations of intent and strong resolve, I don't know what is.

A declared goal is only words until it is translated into overt action. A written goal is little more than scribblings on a piece of paper unless it provokes purposeful labor. The real proof of the validity of a goal or the plan is in the application.

I like the work ethic and competitive spirit of the young heroine in the following *Sports Illustrated* account:

> The University Lake high school girls' basketball team from Hartland, Wisconsin—yep, that state again—was playing Shoreland Lutheran High in Kenosha recently. Four University Lake players were out sick with the flu, leaving only five to suit up. Still, the Lakers led 22–11 at halftime.
>
> Soon, however, University Lake started to recede. Mary Allen fouled out, and the Lakers finished the third quarter with four players and a 25–16 lead. Rita Landis sprained an ankle and departed early in the fourth quarter. Sandy Saeger fouled out with less than three minutes left. And Ann Yeomans fouled out with about one minute to go; but her team still led 33–25. That left Laura Merisalo, who had four fouls, to play against five Shoreland opponents, a problem on defense certainly but also a headache when she had to inbound the ball (she tossed it to an opponent and tried to steal it back).
>
> Laura gave up four points in that final minute, but University Lake still won 33–29.[21]

Laura's goal was to win that game despite the growing adversity and overwhelming odds. So she worked and played hard right up to the victorious end—she was not to be denied!

Step 7: *Verify your goals for monitoring purposes.* To verify is to establish the accuracy or reality of something. For example, someone traveling toward a distant city will stop periodically and check his position on the road map. He may also look at his wristwatch to determine possible time of arrival. These assessments are made to verify location, rate of travel, and other vital aspects of his travel plan.

The same applies to the goal setter and goal striver. He too must monitor his progress and make appropriate adjustments along the way. Once in a while unexpected illness may alter or delay a person's plans. Sometimes favorable winds at his back may accelerate progress ahead of schedule. Therefore it is imperative that the young and youthful verify their positions in relationship to avowed purposes and initiate appropriate changes or course corrections.

A word or two of warning should be added: Don't downgrade your goal or make concessions in your plans to the extent that goals become too soft—too low. Don't take the easy way out. Additionally, don't be hesitant to upgrade your intent when you feel greater stretching and reaching seems right, especially when you have experienced unforeseen blessings and the aid of unseen powers. Be flexible, but don't be compromising to the extent that principles are sacrificed and worthy intent is lost.

Sandtraps of Goal Setting

Elder Dean L. Larsen wrote: "Setting goals and objectives to guide one's efforts can be demonstrated to yield positive results. It is a process, however, that can also be restricting and limiting when it is distorted or misguided. It is important to hold this process in the right perspective when we seek an understanding of the principles that lead to human progress."[22]

In the hope that you will maintain the right perspective in goal setting and goal striving, I offer these words of caution:

Goals must not reflect impure motives or selfish desire. One specialist in human behavior wrote: "Striving for goals which are important to you, not as status symbols, but because they are consistent with your own deep inner wants, is healthful. Striving for real success—for *your* success—through creative accomplishment, brings a deep inner satisfaction. Striving for a phony success to please others brings a phony satisfaction."[23]

Some people "pad" the record and push aside people and principles, all in the name of goal setting and goal striving. Such behavior leads to ultimate failure and hollow, pseudo successes. The motives undergirding your goals must be pure, and the actions directed toward achieving goals must be Christian and in full harmony with the general purposes of your life.

Goals must stir a feeling of competition with self, not others. They should be self-set and self-carried-out. They should help to motivate you to live on a higher level or to do a better thing. Said Elder Boyd K. Packer: "In the eyes of the Lord, everyone may be a winner. Now it is true that we must earn it; but if there is competition in His work, it is not with another soul—it's with our own former selves."[24]

President Kimball adds: "We ascertain and establish acceptable standards of excellence in a given field and measure our work accordingly. We should be less interested in excelling others but more concerned with excelling our own past records and using our established ideal standards and perfection as our goals and the measurement of our attainments and our degree of progress."[25]

Sometimes you will play or work with others in competitive settings. And sometimes that competition may pull you toward a higher level of performance. It may also win you recognition, acclaim, and other rewards. But in the end the "real" competition—the competition that really matters—is the competition that causes you to refine character, grow in knowledge, polish personality, and become a better man or woman.

Goals must not be too rigid or be approached in a mechanistic manner. Overly rigid goals can, in certain circumstances, cause you to turn a deaf ear to the promptings of the Holy Spirit and to overlook spontaneous opportunities. I am not suggesting that a goal be of a "wishy-washy-watery" variety. This type is useless. But I do feel that goals must be analyzed frequently and adjusted occasionally to accord with inspiration received and changes of circumstances.

Goals that are too loose are like a moving target, and the goal striver is made to feel that he is trying to saddle a horse on a fast trot. On the other hand, if the goals are inflexible all possibilities for the application of new insights and recently received inspiration will be thwarted.

Goals must not be set as a means of forcing divine will or offending human agency. I know of a missionary who nearly lost his testimony because he and his companion failed to realize a baptismal goal of a certain number of people in a given month. He contended that they had prayed about the number, felt good about it, presented it to the Lord, and received the Lord's confirmation. When they fell short of the mark, he blamed God for the shortfall.

You must not conclude that you can arbitrarily fix a number in your head and automatically realize it. This is particularly true when you are dealing with spiritual matters and with people, who have their agency. To do so, I fear, under most circumstances is to ask for "that which is contrary to [God's] will."[26]

Goals must be matched by righteous desire, else they prove to be simply so many words written on a page or spoken. If your goal is New York, and if you are the automobile, *desire* is the power that will propel you toward your intended destination. Said the prophet Alma: "I know that [God] granteth unto men according to their desire . . . according to their wills."[27]

It is a high resolve—the heart's desire—that brings fulfillment to the requests from the lips of a young man or woman.[28] A common expression says that where there is a will there is a way. This seems to be the case in most instances. Heartfelt desire makes up for a lot of deficiencies; strong will often overcomes what appears to be overwhelming odds. And when good intent, plans, desire, honest effort, endurance, and so forth, are combined properly by a goal setter/goal striver, many notable things may be accomplished.

In the words of Edgar A. Guest:

> You are the fellow that has to decide
> Whether you'll do it or toss it aside. . . .
> Whether you'll try for the goal that's afar
> Or just be contented to stay where you are.[29]

Few things in life are more exhilarating or motivating than the attainment of a worthwhile goal. It stirs positive thinking ("I can succeed"), encourages the establishment of higher standards or expectations ("I can do more and better work"), and builds self-esteem ("I am a successful person").

Remember, a goal setter is one who obtains a mental view of where he wants to go and of how to get there. He plans; he sets expectations for himself; and he moves forward with purpose and high resolve. He does not wilt in the face of adversity, nor does he entertain thoughts of giving up before the end, because his views of the future are glorious. He repels blindness of mind with that marvelous light that comes into the soul of one who has enough faith in God and self to declare, "I can do all things through Christ which strengtheneth me."[30]

Notes

1. Thomas S. Monson, "Which Road Will You Travel?" *Ensign,* November 1976, p. 51.

2. Mormon 5:18.

3. Spencer W. Kimball, *The Miracle of Forgiveness* (Salt Lake City: Bookcraft, 1969), p. 234.

4. Carlos E. Asay, *In the Lord's Service* (Salt Lake City: Deseret Book Co., 1992), pp. 113–15.

5. *In the Lord's Service,* p. 106.

6. *Webster's New World Dictionary,* p. 598.

7. Earl Nightingale, in "Points to Ponder," *Reader's Digest,* August 1982, p. 135.

8. Moses 1:39.

9. JST Matthew 5:50.

10. *The Teachings of Ezra Taft Benson* (Salt Lake City: Bookcraft, 1988), p. 384.

11. Regional Representatives Seminar, April 1975, p. 8.

12. *The Teachings of Spencer W. Kimball,* Edward L. Kimball, ed. (Salt Lake City: Bookcraft, 1982), p. 474.

13. Proverbs 29:18.

14. See 2 Nephi 1:24.

15. See D&C 9:8–9; 8:2–3; 6:22–24.

16. Ward Cantrell; source unidentified.

17. See Moroni 10:8–19; D&C 46:8–30; 1 Corinthians 12:8–11.

18. See Moses 3:5–7.

19. D&C 3:2.

20. Abraham 3:17.

21. *Sports Illustrated,* February 13, 1978.

22. Dean L. Larsen, "Some Thoughts on Goal-Setting," *Ensign,* February 1981, p. 62.

23. Maxwell Maltz, *Psycho-Cybernetics* (New York: Pocket Books, 1969), pp. 146–47.

24. *Ensign,* May 1975, p. 106.

25. *The Teachings of Spencer W. Kimball,* p. 488.

26. See Helaman 10:4–5; 2 Nephi 4:35.

27. Alma 29:4.

28. See Psalm 21:2.

29. Edgar A. Guest, "You," in *The Light of Faith* (Chicago: Reilly and Lee, 1926), p. 133.

30. Philippians 4:13.

CHAPTER 2

To Avoid Blindness of Mind—
Cultivate Personal Gifts and Talents and Share Them with Others

*E*lder Richard L. Evans expressed himself eloquently on the profitable use of our time and talents:

> Somewhere the story is told of a talented girl who seemed not to be doing enough with the gifts and abilities that she had been given, and under some strong impulse her mother one day impatiently shook her and, in substance, said: "I've given you life. Now you do something with it!" We could conceive of the Father of us all saying about the same: "I've given you life. Now make the most of it! I've given you time, opportunity, talent, intelligence, the good earth and all it offers—now use it, do something with it!" This brings to mind a line, not often heard or said these days, but much full of meaning: "We are not here to play, to dream, to drift." One of the most wasteful wastes in the world is the waste of time, of talent, of opportunity, of creative effort—indiffer-

ence to development, indifference to learning, indifference
to work—the don't-care, drop-out, what's-the-use attitude.
There are times for preparation, and times for serious, responsible performance, and we had better be finding direction, finding ourselves, and moving forward, avoiding in-
different drifting or wasteful delay in using the priceless
abilities and opportunities God has given. One of the
steadying factors in this broad and blessed land, and in each
one's life—one that would reduce restlessness and discon-
tent—would be for all of us to make commitment to develop and use in more useful ways the best of our abilities,
perhaps with a sense that the Father of us all might somehow, sometime shake us, and unforgettably say (which he
has, in more ways than we seem to be aware): "I have given
you life. Now, make the most of it!"[1]

Bob's Story—"Know Thyself"

"I am no good. I have nothing to offer others. I'm just a social parasite." These words were spoken by a young man we
will call Bob. Bob had experienced only limited success in his
youth. More than once he had fallen short of the mark, at least
by his own standards. Others had added to his distress by ridi-
culing him on several occasions.

A loving leader refused to accept Bob's admission of defeat.
It was his feeling that the young man possessed unique talents
that had been blanketed by years of half-hearted efforts, condi-
tioned failure, and constant self-denigration. Like all good leaders, he believed in the worth of every soul and knew that it was
his task to help his young associate understand this truth: "The
greatest battle of life is fought out within the silent chambers of
the soul. A victory on the inside of a man's heart is worth a hundred conquests on the battlefields of life. To be master of yourself is the best guarantee that you will be master of the situation. Know thyself. The crown of character is self-control."[2]

Through a series of interviews, the leader learned that Bob
had the secret ambition to become a distance runner on some
university track team. The leader did not scoff at the idea even
though it came as a surprise. He wisely decided to withhold

judgment and put Bob to the test. The necessary arrangements were made to give the young man a tryout—a tryout to determine whether talents were observable. And they were! Those who watched on the sidelines during the trial run were pleasantly surprised by the youth's long stride, smooth gait, and strong endurance. All marvelled at the performance and felt certain that serious conditioning and training would make Bob a winner.

Excitement began to grow within the young man as he set some goals under the direction of his leader/coach. A training routine was agreed upon. Daily records of the early morning workouts were kept. And good things began to happen. Lethargy was replaced by enthusiasm; the attitude "I'm no good" was replaced by an optimistic "I know I can" mind-set of the young man, as he grew in confidence and as he was fed by the encouragement of others.

In due time the running success spilled over into other phases of the young man's life. His personality blossomed and he found new interests and personal gifts above and beyond that of running a footrace. Success by success he became more independent in his behavior until he emerged as a "real" contributor. The one-time parasite eventually became a vine of spiritual strength to all the "branches" attached to him.

What Is Man?

God has given you life. And it is quite probable that he gave you a charge as you left your heavenly home—a charge that may have included such words as these: "Now, make the most of your experience in mortality. Don't waste your time, talents, or opportunities!"

Whenever I think of the possibilities of today's youth, my mind turns to these inspired words of the psalmist:

What is man, that thou art mindful of him? . . .

For thou hast made him a little lower than the angels, and hast crowned him with glory and honour.

Thou madest him to have dominion over the works of thy hands; thou hast put all things under his feet.[3]

If you were made a little lower than the angels, crowned with glory and honour, and given dominion over the works of God, you surely must have been endowed with a special flair for something. I refer to flairs or natural abilities that are distinctive and that set you apart from others in some wonderful way. I refer to spiritual and physical powers within you just waiting to be tapped. Moreover, I refer to that creative genius bestowed upon you by the great creator who declared all things he made, including you, as being "very good."[4]

Shakespeare had Hamlet declare: "What a piece of work is a man! How noble in reason! How infinite in faculty! In form and moving how express and admirable! In action how like an angel! In apprehension how like a god! The beauty of the world! The paragon [model of perfection] of animals! And yet, to me, what is this quintessence [purest essence] of dust?"[5]

You are a special piece of work! You have been made only a little lower than the angels! You must therefore make the commitment to develop and use the best of your abilities in enriching your life and the lives of others! Don't wait to be shocked or shaken into activity. Take the lead in finding direction, finding yourself, and moving forward toward desirable ends—just as Bob did.

Seek Gifts

Perhaps you have wondered where you were when the gifts and talents were distributed. You may even feel that you were absent from the heavenly distribution center or completely overlooked as the endowments were portioned out. At times I have envied the talents of others and wondered why I didn't receive a greater share. But as I have studied this subject and my knowledge of temporal and spiritual gifts has increased, I have repented of past feelings, for I now know that "to every man [and woman] is given a gift by the Spirit of God."[6] I also know that every man and woman *has* his or her own gift of God.[7] Furthermore, I now know that some may be given an abundance of gifts.[8]

Gifts are not cast freely into the wind. They must be sought, they must be cultivated, they must be used to benefit others—for that is the condition upon which they are granted. Always bear in mind that they are reserved for those who love God and keep his commandments.

Is it possible that a gift lies dormant within you? Perhaps you haven't mined deeply enough within the recesses of your soul to discover the "gold" that resides there. Maybe you haven't heeded sufficiently the subtle intimations of the Spirit which provide clues to special and inner powers.

Important Questions

Soon after my release from the mission field, I wondered about the vocation or profession that I should pursue. I wanted a work that would be interesting, self-fulfilling, one that would enable me to make a contribution to society. I therefore went to the counselling center at the university and took a battery of tests that included aptitude, interest, personality, and other evaluations. After the results of the tests had been tabulated, a specialist sat down with me to interpret the data. He was quick to point out that my profile showed that I should become an "itinerant preacher." Both of us agreed that I should allow more time to lapse and complete my post-mission adjustment before reaching a decision about my lifetime work.

Nonetheless, the testing experience caused me to ask myself important questions, such as:
- What special interest do I possess?
- What type of work do I enjoy most?
- What talents or abilities seem to surface as I deal with others?
- How may I make a proper living, support a family, and find time to serve others?
- What work will provide me with a challenge and cause me to grow?
- What work will prepare me best for eternity?

These and similar probing questions, along with some exploratory work experiences, caused me to ponder and pray about my future. Eventually the Red Sea waters of doubt and indecision parted and the way opened up before me, just as it will for you if you make an honest effort.

Precious time and energy can be wasted if, in the probing for gifts, a person is not perfectly honest with himself. I have heard it said: "You can't lead a cavalry charge if you think you look funny on a horse. If you *do* think you look funny on a horse, then postpone the charge." I would add, sell the horse, forget the charge, and seek to lead out in some other way that matches your personality and interest.

"Bobby, What You Have Is Enough"

There is wisdom in the story that Dr. Robert K. Thomas, the former Academic Vice President of Brigham Young University, tells about his struggle to find his place in life. Early on, he decided that he would become a professional boxer. He was large in stature and seemed to possess all the qualities needed to become a world champion. Fortunately, however, he heard the "wake-up" bell through a retired pugilist who taught him a painful but impressive lesson. After suffering a humiliating beating at the hands of the old fighter, Robert returned home defeated in both body and spirit and complained to his mother about his lack of talent. His wise and loving mother comforted him by saying, "Oh, Bobby, what you *have* is enough!"[9]

What a pity it would have been if Robert Thomas had not been forced to forsake his boxing dream! It was through defeat that he gained victory because he wouldn't give up. One door was closed abruptly in his face; but he sought another door for the release of his special talents. In time, he was moved in the direction of writing, teaching, and other academic pursuits where greater gifts were discovered and used to bless the lives of thousands.

The same can be said about you. Whatever you have is enough, providing you buckle down and use to full advantage that which God has given you. When the wind of adversity strikes your ship, tighten your sails and attend your course, as Bob Thomas did. Your reward will be the discovery of true direction in your life.

Recognizing and Developing Talents

If your talents come incognito (not easily known), as one writer suggested, here are some things that you should understand:

1. "Recognize that there are many kinds of talents" (physical, mental, social, and spiritual).
2. "Recognize your uniqueness."
3. "Recognize Heavenly Father's hand in your abilities."
4. "Recognize that discovering gifts takes time."
5. "Recognize that there are different levels of development."
6. "Recognize that the best talents are available to all."[10]

Once you have recognized a talent, what must be done? You must not neglect it or allow it to go undeveloped, otherwise you may lose it. You must not be afraid to express it or share it with others. And you must not be content with partial development or casual expression of the talent. Said Thomas Wolfe: "If a man has a talent and cannot use it, he has failed. If he has a talent and uses only half of it, he has partly failed. If he has a talent and learns somehow to use the whole of it, he has gloriously succeeded, and won a satisfaction and triumph few men know."[11]

"What we use flourishes," remarked Hippocrates. "What we don't use wastes away." This is readily observed in the use of physical skills, where muscles atrophy quickly and coordination is lost in a few days through inactivity. Yet it applies to all the other gifts, talents, and capacities extended us.

Whenever the development of personal talents is discussed among Latter-day Saints, the stories of Heber J. Grant learning to play baseball and learning to sing almost always surface. Apparently Heber's talents for throwing a ball and singing on key were hidden deep within his soul, even to the extent that few believed he could ever achieve in doing either. Yet he made up his mind that he would develop both talents. He believed in himself, and he followed an adage of Ralph Waldo Emerson's that reads: "That which we persist in doing becomes easier for us to do. Not that the nature of the thing itself is changed, but

that our power to do is increased." President Grant awakened
the latent talents within him.

Spiritual Gifts

Special mention should be made of spiritual gifts. I say this
because when you ignore the spiritual dimensions of your soul,
you bind yourself with the weaknesses of the flesh. But when
you recognize the divine spark within and allow that spark to
be kindled by heavenly fires, almost limitless powers are unleashed. Moses did not become the great deliverer until spiritual powers were ignited within him; Joseph Smith, the young
farm boy, did not become the prophet of the Restoration until
he sought light and truth; and we will never rise to saintly
heights until we seek gifts that will magnify our physical, mental, and spiritual capacities.

We find in holy writ more than a casual invitation to obtain
spiritual gifts. We are told to desire spiritual gifts, to seek
earnestly the best gifts, to lay hold upon every good gift, and to
apply ourselves to our own special gift.[12]

What are those gifts that you should seek earnestly, lay hold
upon, covet earnestly, desire, zealously pursue, apply unto, and
request of God? Specific mention of some fourteen gifts of the
Spirit is made in three scriptural sources. These gifts range from
"To know that Jesus Christ is the Son of God" to gifts of healing,
prophecy, speaking in tongues, and other manifestations of the
Spirit.[13]

I fear that too many young people have the mistaken notion
that spiritual gifts are reserved for old people and are not to be
sought until one is grey with age. Cast this fallacy out of your
mind. Since the beginning of time, several young persons have
been blessed with special powers and abilities in the fulfillment
of assigned missions. Jesus, David, Samuel, Mormon, and
Joseph Smith are cases in point, to name only a few.

Where do these spiritual gifts come from? Elder Marion G.
Romney taught: "The gifts of the Spirit are given by the power
of the Holy Ghost. Without the gift of the Holy Ghost, the manifestations of his gifts may not be enjoyed."[14] Hence, you must

court the influence of the Holy Spirit in all you do, so that you may discover and develop spiritual gifts.

Why are spiritual gifts given? Simply answered, the gifts are given for your benefit and the benefit of all the children of God.[15]

It would be well for you to study the parable of the talents, as taught by the Savior. In that parable a man gave one of his servants five talents, another servant two, and a third servant one talent. Then the man went away for a season. Upon his return, he asked for an accounting of the money or talents he had entrusted to his servants. The one who received five talents had gained five more. The one who received two had gained two more. But the last servant, he who received only one talent, had hid his talent in the earth and gained nothing. In the end, the two who used and multiplied their talents were blessed. The unprofitable servant, however, was chastised and banished from the presence of his master.[16]

There is fair warning in the parable of the talents. You too have been given an endowment or endowments of some sort. Perhaps your allotment is many; perhaps it is only one. The issue is: What have you done or what are you doing with that which has been given you?

In the eyes of God, full performance is preferred over partial performance; work sped up is preferred over work slowed down; forward movement is preferred over steps taken backward. Therefore, God expects you to use gifts, multiply talents, and prove yourself as a profitable servant.

I believe that the acquiring of spiritual gifts is much like learning languages. It may be difficult to learn the second language, but the third and fourth come faster. Why? Because the rudiments of learning languages are much the same, and the mastery of one gives you the edge in mastering another. So it is with spiritual gifts. One gift attunes you to another and enables you to add one upon another until you have gained many spiritual powers.

A Charge to the Gifted

Some years ago Elder Boyd K. Packer charged gifted people in the community of the Saints to lead out in the arts. He said:

> Go to, then, you who are gifted: cultivate your gift. Develop it in any of the arts and in every worthy example of them. If you have the ability and the desire, seek a career or employ your talent as an avocation or cultivate it as a hobby. But in all ways bless others with it. Set a standard of excellence. Employ it in the secular sense to every worthy advantage, but never use it profanely. Never express your gift unworthily. Increase our spiritual heritage in music, in art, in literature, in dance, in drama.
>
> When we have done it our activities will be a standard to the world. And our worship and devotion will remain as unique from the world as the Church is different from the world. Let the use of your gift be an expression of your devotion to Him who has given it to you. We who do not share in it will set a high standard of expectation: "For of him unto whom much is given much is required." (D&C 82:3.)[17]

* * *

Ralph Waldo Emerson believed: "Talent for talent's sake is a bauble and a show. Talent working with joy in the cause of universal truth lifts the possessor to new power as a benefactor."[18] A talent or gift, then, should not be regarded as an end in and of itself. It must be seen as a means to an end—an end that is noble and worthy of achieving.

One who knows that he is a child of God and that he was made "a little lower than the angels" understands that there are marvelous powers within him waiting to be unleashed. These powers include musical talents, poetic rhythm, hand-and-eye coordination, speaking abilities, gifts of language, creative genius, spiritual insights, athletic prowess, and a host of other so-called natural endowments. The person of faith also knows that he must not neglect these inner gifts. Therefore he meditates upon these things, these gifts, and gives himself wholly to them so that they may be developed and ultimately used to benefit himself and others. In the process, blindness of mind is put to flight by the exceeding faith that comes to those who fan the spark of divinity given them by the "Father of spirits."[19]

Notes

1. Richard L. Evans, "The Spoken Word," July 27, 1969; see *Improvement Era,* October 1969, p. 77.

2. Authorship unknown.

3. Psalm 8:4–6.

4. Moses 2:31.

5. *Hamlet,* 2.2. 315–20.

6. D&C 46:11.

7. See 1 Corinthians 7:7.

8. See D&C 46:29.

9. *New Era,* October 1972, p. 42.

10. Anya Bateman, "If Your Talents Come Incognito," *Ensign,* June 1991, pp. 62–65.

11. In John Bartlett, *Familiar Quotations* (Boston: Little, Brown and Co., 1968), p. 1049.

12. See 1 Corinthians 14:1; D&C 46:8; 1 Corinthians 12:31; Moroni 10:30; D&C 8:4.

13. See *In the Lord's Service,* pp. 123–24; see also D&C 46:8–30; Moroni 10:8–24; 1 Corinthians 12:1–11.

14. Conference Report, April 1956, p. 72.

15. See D&C 46:26; Romans 1:11.

16. See Matthew 25:14–30.

17. Boyd K. Packer, "The Arts and the Spirit of the Lord," *Ensign,* August 1976, pp. 60–65.

18. In Edmund Fuller, ed., *Thesaurus of Quotations* (New York: Crown Publishers, 1941), p. 884.

19. Psalm 8:4–6; Hebrews 12:9; see also 1 Timothy 4:14–16.

CHAPTER 3

To Avoid Blindness of Mind—
Select Righteous Role Models and Follow Their Examples

*I*t was wartime, and German U-boats were searching the sea for Allied ships to sink. One of them found such a target on February 3, 1943—the United States troopship S.S. *Dorchester*, carrying about nine hundred people, including six hundred servicemen. When the torpedo found its mark, the ship began to sink rapidly. In twenty minutes it would be gone.

Four different religious faiths were represented in the four army chaplains aboard—Alex Goode, Clark Poling, George Fox, and John Washington. These four men, who had become close friends during the voyage, sprang into action when the torpedo hit. They prayed with the men, they helped in handing out rafts and life jackets, and when the supply of these was exhausted they took off their own life jackets and put them on four young soldiers.

Some two hundred people survived. From their rafts many of them observed the chaplains standing on the deck, arms linked, praying as the ship went down.

Heroes—People at Their Best

Chaplains Goode, Poling, Fox, and Washington were real war heroes. They were men of great strength and towering courage who willingly gave their lives that others might live. Such display of love for their fellow soldiers was spontaneous, not practiced or rehearsed. Hence we can conclude that their sacrificing example was more a reflection of Christ-like character than it was a fulfillment of military duty. Their heroic actions will long be remembered, not only because a commemorative chapel was erected in their honor but also because many of the survivors and others who heard later of the account were inspired by these four righteous role models.

Speaking of "this generation" or youth of today and their heroes, a respected educator said:

> Young people do not assimilate the values of their group by learning words (truth, justice, etc.) and their definitions. They learn attitudes, habits, and ways of judging. They learn these in intensely personal transactions with their immediate family or associates. They learn them in the routines and crises of living, but they also learn them through songs, stories, drama, and games. They do not learn ethical principles; they emulate ethical or unethical people. They do not analyze or list the attributes they wish to develop; they identify with people who seem to them to have these attributes. That is why young people need models, both in their imaginative life and in their environment, models of what man at his best can be.[1]

Two Important E-Words

To understand Gardner's point of view about "this generation" and youth's need for role models, you must know the meaning of two words, *emulate* and *ethical*. *Emulate* means to imitate or try to equal or surpass someone else. *Ethical* refers to principles or people that conform to high moral standards. It is Gardner's feeling that young people imitate good or bad people with whom they have intense personal contacts; that they do not acquire ethical or unethical behaviors simply by reading books, memorizing definitions of words, and listing attributes.

There are too many young people who grow up in environments where the drug pushers, peddlers of sex, and other immoral individuals become the desired role models. In such places the youth become blinded to the differences between good and bad—ethical and unethical. They live with the illusion that sex equates with adulthood, that participation in gang violence is a badge of honor, and drug dealing is the means of becoming prosperous and secure. Consequently some young men and women select role models of what man at his worst can be and, emulating them, reap the bitter consequences.

Those who emulate the unethical role model will be even as "when an hungry man dreameth, and, behold, he eateth; but he awaketh, and his soul is empty; or as when a thirsty man dreameth, and, behold, he drinketh; but he awaketh, and, behold, he is faint, and his soul hath appetite."[2]

On the other hand, those who emulate the ethical role model will not come up empty or faint, for the ethical "hero (heroine) is one who kindles a great light in the world, who sets up blazing torches in the dark streets of life for men to see by."[3] Most clear-thinking and informed people agree with that profound statement and this one: "All young people need [worthy] heroes to emulate. There is no life of the mind or aspiration of the spirit without emulation of great heroes. . . . Our [youth] must feel at times that they are in the company of a great human spirit."[4]

Role Models from Imaginative Life

Gardner alludes to two types of role models: those taken from our imaginative life and those who live among us in our immediate environment. The one is of the past and may be found in history and other books, particularly the scriptures. The other is of the present and may be found in our families or among our circle of friends and associates. Both types are desirable and, if they are models of what men and women at their best can be, serve as a light and pattern for the impressionable young.

We read of the many heroes or heroines of history, such as a Madame Curie, a Florence Nightingale, an Abraham Lincoln, a George Washington, a Christopher Columbus, and others. All of these people had their share of weaknesses because they were mortals. But all of them exemplified virtues well worth emulation by the youth of all generations. What young man or woman would go wrong imitating the courage of a Joan of Arc, the integrity of a Washington, or the faith and vision of a Columbus? Each in his or her own way serves as a beacon of hope to the aspiring youth who want to make something good of their own lives.

I wish all young women would emulate the loyalty and commitment of a Ruth,[5] the sense of destiny of an Esther,[6] the depth of testimony of a Martha,[7] and the love of God such as Mary showed.[8] Just imagine what a young lady might become if she sought diligently to acquire all the virtues associated with the great women mentioned in holy writ.

Similarly, should not young men strive to become a composite of all the heroes mentioned in the scriptures? There were Samuel, Ezra, Peter, Paul, Nephi, Moroni, and many others who possessed virtues that never wither with age or become out of date. Of Moroni it is written: "If all men had been, and were, and ever would be, like unto Moroni, behold, the very powers of hell would have been shaken forever; yea, the devil would never have power over the hearts of the children of men."[9] The same could be said of the others who were "good soldier[s] of Jesus Christ"[10] and ethical role models worthy of emulation.

Role Models from Real Life

Role models taken from our imaginative lives do have their places. They can, however, become very impersonal and sometimes unbelievable, thus losing their magic influence upon our dreams and aspirations. In history books we read about great heroes; but they are still far removed from the more believable here-and-now scene. We read of heroines in stories, songs, poems, and even in scriptures; yet they lived at other times and in other places and under other circumstances, making them seem less personal and credible than heroes and heroines should be. So in addition to the role models of our imaginations, you need to select real-life role models—men and women you can see with your own eyes, hear with your own ears, and on occasions touch with your own hands.

President Spencer W. Kimball endorsed that need when he quoted Walter MacPeek: "Boys need lots of heroes like Lincoln and Washington. But they also need to have some heroes close by. They need to know some man of towering strength and basic integrity personally. They need to meet him on the street, to hike and camp with him, to see him close to home, every day, [in] down-to-earth situations; to feel close enough to him to ask questions and to talk things over man-to-man with him."[11]

The same applies to young women. When a girl watches an older heroine achieve a lofty work she is reminded that tasks are doable and that goals are reachable. The younger one is heard to declare as she points to the older, "She did it! I can do the same."

Thomas Jefferson, the author of the Declaration of Independence and one who was influential with the founding fathers of the United States, wrote the following about his youth and the indebtedness he felt to good role models:

> I had the good fortune to become acquainted very early with some characters of very high standing, and to feel the incessant wish that I could ever become what they were. Under temptations and difficulties, I would ask myself— what would [those people] do in this situation? What course is it will assure me their approbation? I am certain that this mode of deciding on my conduct tended more to correctness than any reasoning power I possessed. Knowing the even and dignified line they pursued, I could never doubt for a moment which of two courses would be in character for them, whereas, seeking the same object through a process of moral reasoning, and with the jaundiced eye of youth, I should have often erred.[12]

The eyes of youth are jaundiced in many respects. That is, their views can become colored or clouded by the lack of experience, insight, and understanding. So to avoid making foolish mistakes you must fix your eyes upon those who are older, whose eyes are not jaundiced, and who have already walked "the even and dignified line." And you must feel deeply the "incessant wish" to become just as worthy and just as righteous as your role models are or were.

I wish all young people could have a role model like the one I had in my youth. He was a few years older than I, yet he inspired me in many ways. Dale was tall and handsome; he was a star athlete, the drum major of the school band, a scholar, and one who held to high moral standards. He caused me to develop the "incessant wish" to become like him. Is it any wonder that I attempted to follow in his footsteps by participating in sports, in the high school band, in taking my studies seriously, and in serving a full-time mission? He was like a North Star to me. I knew I would not lose my direction if I kept my eyes upon him.

Sometimes the greatest heroes and heroines in our lives are so close to us that we either overlook them or take them for granted. I'm thinking of the invalid who struggles and suffers in silence without complaint. I'm thinking of the mother who goes without a new dress so that a daughter may have a new formal for the junior prom. I'm thinking of the father who forgoes a vacation, a new car, or a new roof on the house so that a son may have money to serve a mission or attend college. These and others like them are the "real," real-life heroes and heroines of our day worthy of your admiration and emulation.

In a general conference address, President Howard W. Hunter remarked:

> Surely we need not look far to see the unnoticed and forgotten heroes of daily life. I am speaking of those you know and those I know who quietly and consistently do the things they ought to do. I am talking about those who are always there and always willing. I am referring to the uncommon valor of the mother who—hour after hour, day and night—will stay with and care for a sick child, or the invalid who struggles and suffers without complaint. I'm including those

who always volunteer to give blood or volunteer to work with Scouts. I am thinking of those who may not be mothers but who nevertheless "mother" the children of the world. I am speaking of those who are always there to love and nurture.[13]

A Disappointing Study

I read of a study made at one of the more prestigious universities in the United States. The study was designed to find answers to two questions: (1) Do young people have heroes or heroines, after whom they pattern their lives? And (2) if they do, who are they? Results of the study were disappointing on both counts. Only 23 percent of the 1205 students polled had identified role models. Those who did have role models listed most frequently as their ideal a politician with an immoral and unethical reputation. A professional boxer of a tarnished character was on the list. But most disappointing of all, Jesus Christ received only three votes, tying with an actress, a stunt car daredevil, and a Russian writer. Men like Einstein, Thoreau, Beethoven, Washington, Jefferson, Lincoln, and other notables were barely mentioned.

It is true what one leader said about some of today's heroes with clay feet who are leading many young people down strange roads and toward certain disaster: "The heroes or superstars in the sports and entertainment world, and there are many, frequently become examples of dishonesty, instability, and infidelity. They flagrantly and indifferently flaunt those weaknesses of character and immorality before a doting and accepting world, as Korihor said, 'according to the management of the creature.'"[14]

Youth's hunger for heroes and heroines is exemplified by the fact that the rooms of most adolescents are adorned with posters of rock musicians, athletes, and movie stars. Perhaps some of these celebrities possess a virtue or two. But should "greatness" be measured by performance on the stage or the basketball court? What kind of a role model should you hold up as your personal ideal?

A Word of Warning—Sam's Story

As you select role models and follow their examples, a word of warning seems appropriate. No one is perfect; Jesus was the only sinless person to live upon this earth. However, there are people who possess certain characteristics or virtues worth emulation. It is upon these good things seen in others that you should focus your attention. You must therefore be careful that you choose heroes or heroines who really possess virtues, not virtueless models with "clay feet" who crumble or collapse under close scrutiny. The "clay feet" variety often disillusion and disappoint admirers when their behavior is inconsistent and falls short of expectations; and, much as an incorrect road map does, they lead the impressionable young down crooked paths.

When Sam was very young, a coach taught him to pole vault and inspired him to become a champion in the sport. Sam practiced long hours with the "incessant hope" that one day he might soar high over the bar like his mentor and become a champion.

Year by year Sam became stronger and faster, winning the pole vaulting event in most high school track meets. He trained hard under the watchful eye of his coach and gained confidence in himself as his skills improved. And even though his coach moved out of the community for business reasons, Sam maintained his desire to excel.

When the regional track meet was held at the close of Sam's junior year, he had reached a high level of performance. His confidence was strong and his determination to come off the winner was centered in the memories of his hero-coach. Just as the competition began, Sam was informed that his coach had arrived back in the city for a brief visit and was in the stands with the other spectators. Sam's excitement soared, and the adrenaline began to flow through his body as he thought of the prospects of winning and then showing his medal to the one who had inspired and tutored him.

Sam not only won his event but he also set a record that would stand for years. He was proud and excited to step on the winner's platform and to accept the award and the applause of the crowd. He was on cloud nine and felt that he was standing on the pinnacle of success. With the medal in hand he rushed to and fro among the people hoping to find his role model and to receive his commendations. But the bubble of joy burst and the victory lost its glitter when he found his coach lying in a drunken stupor in the back seat of an automobile.

The boy was crushed to discover that his hero—his idol—had "clay feet" and was not what he had thought. Sam returned home a disillusioned and brokenhearted young man. Not even his loving parents were able to pull him out of the pit of despair during the night that followed. It wasn't until the next morning that the embarrassed coach sought Sam out, apologized for his actions, and promised that he would never disappoint Sam again.

One should not judge Sam's coach too harshly. After all, he did contribute significantly toward the young man's success; he did acknowledge his error—a heroic action in and of itself; and he did attempt to make things right with his young protégé. You must be very selective in identifying with role models, however, for all are possessed of some human frailties and all have their moments of weakness. Perhaps it is wise and safer to fix one's mind upon the virtues of a hero or heroine and over-look the characteristics that are not worthy of emulation.

In reference to both "imaginative life" and "real life" role models, Conan Doyle offered this sage counsel: "Let us thank God if we have outgrown their vices. Let us pray to God that we may ever hold their virtues."[15]

Goals and Heroes

One of the greatest track stars in history was Jesse Owens, the man who set records in the 100 meters, 200 meters, and broad jump in the 1936 Olympic Games. He spoke often of the importance of setting goals and modeling one's life after heroes or worthy role models. It was his feeling that young people must take four steps in order to achieve goals. They are: (1) build the *determination,* (2) *dedicate* yourself to the task, (3) exercise *self-discipline,* and (4) have the *proper attitude.* In addition to the four steps, it was his contention that aspiring individuals must have eyes fixed upon exemplary role models—role models who have been successful and who have realized their own dreams. "Seeing other people . . . realize their dreams," said Owens, "shows [youth that they] can do it too."[16]

The Ultimate Role Model

I read of a man who attributed his righteous living and his many achievements to his mother and a placard that she placed in his room when he was just a boy. The placard was mounted on the wall in front of the bed so that it was the first thing he saw in the morning as he opened his eyes and the last thing he saw at night before he dropped off to sleep. It read:

> Think no thing Jesus would not think.
> Say no thing Jesus would not say.
> Do no thing Jesus would not do.
> Go no place Jesus would not go.

The loving and caring mother wanted her son to "let virtue garnish [his] thoughts unceasingly";[17] she wanted him "to speak evil of no man";[18] she wanted him to live according to the "golden rule," which is, "Therefore all things whatsoever ye would that men should do to you, do ye even so to them";[19] and she wanted him to stand in holy places and to "abhor that which is evil."[20]

In a sense, the placard served as a shield and a protection for the boy. When he was tempted to entertain unkind thoughts or dirty stories, he remembered the guidelines provided by his mother and carefully screened that which went into his mind. If he was tempted to use profanity or tell a lie, he remembered the warning of his mother and guarded his words. Whenever he was enticed to do the wrong thing, he reflected on the sign and did otherwise. And when others invited him to go into the wrong places, the words on the placard, now registered in his mind and heart, shouted "Stop! Don't go!" Over the course of time his resolve to live as his mother had taught him to live became stronger and stronger, and the temptations to do otherwise became weaker and weaker.

It is obvious that the mother loved her son and wanted him to accept Christ as the ultimate role model—a model without clay feet, one free of any vice, and one who would never disappoint. She may have had this scripture in mind when she prepared the placard:

> As ye have therefore received Christ Jesus the Lord, so walk ye in him:
>
> Rooted and built up in him, and stablished in the faith, as ye have been taught, abounding therein with thanksgiving.
>
> Beware lest any man spoil you through philosophy and vain deceit, after the tradition of men, after the rudiments of the world, and not after Christ.[21]

What youth could go wrong patterning his or her life after the Son of God? What young man or woman could do better than to model his or her life after that of the Great Exemplar, he who invites all to "come and follow me"?[22]

Of the Savior's early years Frederic W. Farrar wrote: "In these years He 'began to do' long before He 'began to teach' (Acts 1:1). They were the years of sinless childhood, a sinless boyhood, a sinless youth, a sinless manhood, spent in that humility, toil, obscurity, submission, contentment, prayer, to make them an eternal example to all our race. . . . It was during these years that His life is for us the main example of how we ought to live. . . .This sovereign Master, who was to teach all virtues, and to point out the way of life, began from His youth up, by sanctifying in His own person the practice of the virtuous life He came to teach."[23]

Jesus was the model of what man at his best can be; he walked the even and dignified line throughout his lifetime; he was the epitome of ethical behavior because he was free of vice and full of virtue; he is as close to home and as down to earth as we will permit him to be; and he is the ultimate role model upon whom all youth should fix their gaze and pin their stars.

"Therefore," said the Savior, "what manner of men [and women] ought ye to be? Verily, I say unto you, even as I am."[24] These words were spoken nearly two thousand years ago, but they are just as relevant today as they were when first spoken. Without question, Jesus is the greatest hero who ever graced this world. His life, his teachings, and his sacrificing example provide inspiration to all who believe in him and who accept him as their Savior, Master, and hero of all heroes.

*   *   *

Look to God; look to Christ; look to the ultimate role models and live. Yes, look to righteous role models, follow their examples, and maintain the "incessant wish" to become like men and women of high standing and noble stature. Such looks and wishes will help you avoid blindness of mind.

There are times when you wonder whether you can accomplish this or that task. When you do so, you allow your faith to sag and you permit blindness of mind to gain the upper hand. But if you fix your eyes upon someone further down the road whose course is set and whose stride is steady in the proper direction, you will be able to regain control and press forward with renewed confidence and vigor. Such heroes or heroines will remind you that the task is doable and you will find yourself saying: "They did it! and I too can do it." Worthy role models are much like a compass to the young. They point the direction, enabling followers to walk through "mists of darkness," avoid pitfalls, and reach desired objectives.[25]

Keep in mind this profound thought as you seek to emulate a moral hero and strive to be one yourself: "The hero [heroine] is one who kindles a great light in the world, who sets up blazing torches in the dark streets of life for men to see by. The saint is the man [woman] who walks through the dark paths of the world, himself [herself] a 'light.'"[26]

Notes

1. John Gardner, *Self-Renewal* (New York: Harper and Row, 1964), p. 124.

2. Isaiah 29:8.

3. Victor L. Brown, Conference Report, October 1963, p. 120.

4. Levi Edgar Young, Conference Report, October 1958, p. 64.

5. Ruth 1:16–18.

6. Esther 4:14–16.

7. John 11:20–27.

8. Matthew 26:6–13.

9. Alma 48:17.

10. 2 Timothy 2:3.

11. Spencer W. Kimball, *Ensign*, May 1975, pp. 79–80.

12. Alf J. Mapp, Jr., *Thomas Jefferson: A Strange Case of Mistaken Identity* (New York: Madison Books, 1987), pp. 22–23.

13. Howard W. Hunter, *Ensign*, May 1982, p. 19.

14. Durrel A. Woolsey, *Ensign*, November 1990, p. 43; see also Alma 30:17.

15. A. Conan Doyle, *The White Company* (New York: Cosmopolitan Book Co., 1922), p. 363.

16. The Salt Lake Tribune, November 12, 1977.

17. D&C 121:45.

18. Titus 3:2.

19. Matthew 7:12.

20. Romans 12:9.

21. Colossians 2:6–8.

22. Matthew 19:21.

23. Frederic W. Farrar, *The Life of Christ* (Salt Lake City: Bookcraft, 1994), pp. 95–96.

24. 3 Nephi 27:27.

25. See 1 Nephi 12:17.

26. Victor L. Brown, Conference Report, October 1963, p. 120.

PART II

To Avoid Hardness of Heart—
Be Obedient and Do Good Works

A few years ago my wife and I were working in our garden when I suffered a heart attack. There was little or no advance warning. Suddenly I broke out in a heavy sweat, my pulse raced, there was a burning in my chest, intense pain enveloped me, and I was overcome with that feeling of impending doom.

I was rushed to the hospital and placed under the watchful care of competent cardiologists. Among other things, the physicians prescribed a change in lifestyle—to a lifestyle that included proper aerobic exercise, a low-fat diet, and a reduction of stress. Having faith in my doctors, I accepted the disciplined measures prescribed and not only recovered from the illness but also enjoyed more abundant living.

It is much the same with those whose spiritual well-being is threatened by hardness of heart. This deadly malady must also be combatted with a change of lifestyle—to a lifestyle free of physical excesses, free of rebellious tendencies, and open to all the "good works" that invite the softening influence of the Holy Spirit.

The Great Physician, Our Lord and Savior, Jesus Christ, has prescribed to all a style of living which centers in three essential actions. They are: (1) "Keep my commandments" (Exodus 20:6), (2) "Honour thy father and thy mother" (Exodus 20:12), and (3) "To every thing there is a season, and a time to every purpose under the heaven" (Ecclesiastes 3:1–2). Those who have believing hearts and trust in God and parents will accept the prescription given and live accordingly. As a consequence, the obedient will enjoy spiritual health and reap many other promises, including prosperity, a long life, and abiding happiness.

Yes, hardness of heart is a deadly condition that takes its toll among the youth. Young people must heed the warning signs at the very onset of this disease and keep the arteries of their souls clean by willfully obeying the laws of God, heeding the counsel of loving parents, and living in harmony with the eternal rhythm of life. Then, and only then, will they avoid hardness of heart, a condition that is damning to the whole soul of man—an illness that has claimed more victims than any plague known to mankind.

CHAPTER 4

To Avoid Hardness of Heart—
Obey God's Commandments

*I*n the following interesting analogy Elder Robert L. Simpson underlined the advantages that come from keeping God's commandments:

> Last Monday night my high-school-age son persuaded me to sit down and watch the second half of a football game. I have always made it a policy that no sacrifice is too great for my boy. So we sat down and watched football. While watching this game, some facts became very apparent. . . .
>
> I noticed, for example, that there were no shortcuts to the goal line. It was a hundred yards in both directions. I also noticed that the team that seemed to have had the most practice, that did the best planning, that executed their plays the best, and that had the best team attitude was the team that made the most points.
>
> I also noticed that when team members cooperated and helped one another, the team made the most yardage.
>
> It was also obvious that when someone broke the rules, there was always a penalty imposed. It sounds a lot like life,

doesn't it? In talking about this to my boy, he said, "Fifteen yards is nothing; but, Dad, when you ground me for three days, that is too much."

We also noticed that no one was allowed to make up his own rules as the game progressed. They all lost their free agency to do that when they agreed to join the team and play according to the established rules.

And last but not least, I noticed when it was all over, the winning team was a lot happier than the team that lost.

. . . We believe that "men are, that they might have joy"; and joy can best come as we obtain victory in the game of life, played according to the only acceptable rules—those set down by our Heavenly Father.[1]

The Case of Pete

Whenever I think of the slippery path of youth and the need to obey God's commandments, I think of a young man whom I shall call Pete. Pete was tall, dark, and handsome. He was also blessed with a keen mind, a strong physical body, and many social graces. Everyone seemed to like Pete, for he was pleasant to be around. Moreover, he was envied by most of his friends because of his athletic prowess. If there was a game to be played, he could play it better than anyone, so he always came away the winner.

At the beginning of his senior year and the basketball season Pete was the talk of the school and community. Everyone felt confident that Pete would lead his team to the state championship.

In the pre-season games, Pete was the highest scorer and the star. Few opponents had players who could stop such a well-coordinated and gifted athlete as Pete. In addition, the spirit and morale of the team grew with each victory, for Pete's strength seemed to build the confidence and pull up the performance of teammates.

When league play began, something awful happened. First, Pete assumed that he was beyond the established rules and began to break training. A concerned coach issued proper warnings. Loving parents and Church leaders pleaded with him to stop his carousing. Loyal friends stepped forward to help him overcome his rebelliousness. However, all the appeals made by the coach, his parents, and friends fell on deaf ears. Pete would not listen to anyone. He felt that he was beyond the rules—they only applied to others. Slowly his heart became more and more hardened and his flaunting of the rules became more and more blatant.

Second, Pete lost the vision of what he could do for himself and the team if he lived properly. His view of the championship, a possible college scholarship, and other future possibilities became clouded over by the fleshly pleasures of the moment. Others tried hard to help him see the error of his ways and to refocus his mind upon previous goals and aspirations. As his heart hardened, however, his mind became blinded, and he lost sight of all the good things he could have become and the good things he could have done.

The team regrouped after Pete's expulsion from the squad and did better than most people expected. No, they didn't win the state championship, but they came very close. Most profited from the mistake made by their former teammate and learned a valuable lesson about the need to obey rules and to keep their eyes fixed on worthy objectives.

Pete eventually became a dropout—he dropped out of school, out of church, out of family, and, later, even out of society. I say society because the breaking of training rules grew into the breaking of civil laws, even to the extent that he committed a gross crime and received a stiff sentence in a state penitentiary.

I weep when I think of Pete and the other young men and women who break the rules that govern the game of life and who become hard of heart. I also think of this statement made by John Greenleaf Whittier:

> Of all sad words of tongue or pen,
> The saddest are these: "It might have been."

Commandments—Expressions of Love

Too many young people regard every "thou shalt" and every "thou shalt not" as God's means of tormenting mankind, especially the youth. They fail to understand that each commandment is really our Heavenly Father's way of saying, "I care," "I love you," and "I want to protect you." If God hated us, he would never issue us a warning; he would allow us to live in a lawless state; and he would laugh as we went sinning, stumbling, and suffering every step of the way. But since he is a loving God of law and order, he provides us with commandments and promises and invites us to walk in faith, thus avoiding the heartaches associated with hardness of heart.

One of the most insightful and oft-quoted statements about commandments and mankind was made by Cecil B. DeMille:

> We are too inclined to think of law as something merely restrictive—something hemming us in. We sometimes think of law as the opposite of liberty. But this is a false conception. . . . God does not contradict himself. He did not create man and then, as an after-thought, impose upon him a set of arbitrary, irritating, restrictive rules. He made man free—and then gave him commandments to keep him free. . . . We cannot break the Ten Commandments. We can only break ourselves against them—or else, by keeping them, rise through them to the fulness of freedom under God. God means us to be free. With divine daring, He gave us the power of choice.[2]

No, you cannot break the commandments. You can, however, break yourself against them when you fail to honor God's unchangeable laws—laws that were given you to help you resist the enemies of your soul. Pete broke himself against the commandments, and so do others who arrogantly feel that they are above the law and who thereby become a law unto themselves. The truth is that our prisons are full of people who thumbed their noses at rules, regulations, laws, and all else that assures us the freedom to come and to go and to live harmoniously with others.

God has written himself and his laws in everything that is around you. Each sign of his existence and each command given is evidence of his love for you. If only your eyes could see and your souls feel all that he has set before you, it would be so much easier to accept his love and to keep his commandments.

Blessing or Curse

I wish all young people would burn one essential truth into their minds and hearts and never forget it. It is: "Behold, I set before you this day a blessing and a curse; a blessing, if ye obey the commandments of the Lord your God . . . and a curse, if ye will not obey the commandments of the Lord your God."[3]

Obedience brings blessings; disobedience brings a curse or loss of blessings. It is as simple and direct as that! And let it be ever understood that God does not lie, nor does he play games with you. When he said, "I, the Lord, am bound when ye do what I say; but when ye do not what I say, ye have no promise,"[4] he meant it. He meant it for Adam; he meant it for you; and he meant it for every person born into this world from the first person to the very last.

When asked why he was obedient in making an offering to the Lord, Adam answered: "I know not, save the Lord commanded me."[5] A man of less faith might have responded, "I am not sure, but if I continue to do so, what is in it for me?" It was not necessary for God to dangle a promised reward before Adam to win his allegiance. Nor should your submission to divine will be predicated solely upon the rewards that come from obeying the commandments.

Nonetheless, there are laws established by a just and loving God. And when those laws are honored, that God of order is bound to share the related merits of those laws with the obedient. For example, below are listed four commandments. Opposite each commandment are the blessings promised to all of those who love the law-giver, who trust in his word, and who are willing to prove him. Other examples could be cited.

Commandment	Promised Blessing
Law of Health— Word of Wisdom	And all saints who remember to keep and do these sayings, walking in obedience to the commandments, shall receive health in their navel and marrow to their bones; And shall find wisdom and great treasures of knowledge, even hidden treasures;

Commandment	Promised Blessing
Law of Health— Word of Wisdom	And shall run and not be weary, and shall walk and not faint. And I, the Lord, give unto them a promise, that the destroying angel shall pass by them, as the children of Israel, and not slay them. Amen.[6]
Honour thy Father and thy Mother	Children, obey your parents in the Lord: for this is right. Honour thy father and mother; (which is the first commandment with promise;) That it may be well with thee, and thou mayest live long on the earth.[7]
Keep the Sabbath Day Holy	And inasmuch as ye do these things with thanksgiving, with cheerful hearts and countenances, not with much laughter, for this is sin, but with a glad heart and a cheerful countenance— Verily I say, that inasmuch as ye do this, the fulness of the earth is yours, the beasts of the field and the fowls of the air, and that which climbeth upon the trees and walketh upon the earth.[8]
Law of Tithing	Bring ye all the tithes into the storehouse, that there may be meat in mine house, and prove me now herewith, saith the Lord of hosts, if I will not open you the windows of heaven, and pour you out a blessing, that there shall not be room enough to receive it. And I will rebuke the devourer for your sakes, and he shall not destroy the fruits of your ground; neither shall your vine cast her fruit before the time in the field, saith the Lord of hosts. And all nations shall call you blessed: for ye shall be a delightsome land, saith the Lord of hosts.[9]

With every commandment there are two certainties: (1) a promised blessing to the obedient; (2) a curse or forfeiture of blessings to the disobedient. It is certain and can be relied upon. The choice is left to the individual.

Standards of Excellence

Far from being a detriment or an uncomfortable restriction, God's law is one of the greatest blessings of life, for it brings us commandments, standards, and discipline without which we would be lost. Elder Richard L. Evans warned:

> If someone tells you, my beloved young friends, that you can set the commandments of God aside without realizing the results—if someone tells you *that*, then you may know that you are listening to someone who doesn't know, or isn't telling you the truth. . . .
> We ought to live as we ought to live, not only because it would please God, not only because it would please our parents, but as a favor for ourselves—for every commandment, every requirement God has given is for *our* happiness, for *our* health, and for *our* peace and progress. O my beloved young friends, even selfishly it is smart to keep the commandments God has given.[10]

Latter-day Saint youth are indeed fortunate to have received from concerned Church leaders a document published in 1990 entitled *For the Strength of Youth*. This inspired booklet contains very specific instructions on dating, dress and appearance, friendshipping, honesty, language, media, mental and physical health, music and dancing, sexual purity, Sunday behavior, repentance, and spiritual help. Of special interest is a paragraph in this booklet answering the question, Why standards?

> Standards are rules or guidelines given to help you measure your conduct. Why has the Lord given standards? He wants all his children to return to live with him one day.

However, he knows that only those who are worthy will be able to live with him. Standards help you know how well you are preparing to live with your Father in Heaven. Your entire lives on earth are intended to give you the opportunity to learn to choose good over evil, service over selfishness, kindness and thoughtfulness over self-indulgence and personal gratification. By comparing your behavior and thoughts with your Father's standards, you are in a better position to govern yourselves and make the right choices. God's commandments (standards) are constant, unwavering, and dependable. As you adhere to them, you will receive countless blessings from heaven—including the gift of eternal life.[11]

A Classic Old Coat

The story is told of a young man whose life was changed dramatically by wearing a classic old coat that was regarded by himself and others as a standard of excellence. It seems that this particular teenager had previously dressed sloppily, approached his schoolwork casually, and took little or no pride in how he looked or in what he did. Such behavior became a grave concern to his parents, teachers, and others who cared for him. One day, however, through rather unusual circumstances, he purchased a coat described as a piece of clothing "bearing that touch of classic elegance" and began wearing it to school. Very quickly he became the envy of his classmates, and to the surprise of those who knew him he began to display a model type of behavior to match the coat. Apparently it was the coat—the standard of excellence—that caused him to be less contrary, more quiet, more judicious, more mannerly, more thoughtful, and more eager to please.

Toward the close of the story, the author states: "There is something to be said for wearing a standard of excellence for the world to see, for practicing standards of excellence in thought, speech and behavior, and for matching what is on the inside to what is on the outside."[12]

Our Dual Nature

What does reside inside of you that should be matched with quality thought, speech, and behavior? Simply stated, it is the "spirit of man,"[13] which is the offspring of Almighty God.[14] God is the Father of our spirits—the father of the "inner" man and woman.[15]

The thoughts you entertain, therefore, the words you speak, and the things you do need to be made to match the one in whose image you were made. Keep in mind that "the spirit and the body are the soul of man."[16] Both parts of your being must be cared for and kept clean, because the pollution of one may contaminate the other. Similarly, the improvement of one will add beauty to the other, just as the classic coat "beautified" the behavior of the young man in the above story.

Every accountable person should remember that "our words will condemn us . . . our works will condemn us . . . and our thoughts will also condemn us," if we do not watch ourselves.[17] At the same time, we should also remember that our words, works, and thoughts will bless us if they are controlled and made to match what is on the inside of us. So, following the admonition of a prophet, "observe the commandments of God, and continue in the faith . . . even unto the end of your lives."[18]

What Are Your "Die Fors" and "Live Fors"?

I read an article about a teacher who urged his students to decide early their "die fors"—things that they would hold on to and preserve at all costs. In his speech he said: "At some point in your career, you will be called upon to do something you find objectionable. You have to decide . . . whether it is also so . . . wrong that you are willing to walk away from the job."[19] Young people without "die fors" or imperative standards of behavior become prey to negative and evil influences, whereas those who have determined well in advance what is unethical or wrong can more effectively withstand unwholesome peer pressures and the tempter's enticing voice.

Elder Spencer W. Kimball in effect equated "die fors" with "This I will not do," and "live fors" with "This I will do." Said he:

> Thus our young people should drive down stakes early, indicating their paths. The stakes are of two kinds: "This I *will* do" and "This I *will not* do." These decisions pertain to general activities, standards, spiritual goals, and personal programs. They should include anticipations for marriage and family. Very early, youth should have been living by a plan. They are the wise young man and the wise young woman who will profit by the experience of others, and who early set a course in their education, a mission, the finding of a pure, clean sweetheart to be a life's companion, their temple marriage and their Church service. When such a course is charted and the goal is set, it is easier to resist the many temptations and to say "no" to the first cigarette, "no" to the first drink, "no" to the car ride which will take one into the dark, lonely and hazardous places, "no" to the first improper advances which lead eventually to immoral practices.[20]

The daughters of Onitah had their "die fors." They were killed upon an altar "because of their virtue; they would not bow down and worship gods of wood or of stone."[21] Similarly, the four children of Israel had their "die fors." Even though threatened with loss of privileges and death in a fiery furnace, they would not defile themselves with the king's meat nor the wine which he drank, nor would they worship golden idols.[22] One other group of young men, known as the sons of Helaman, had their "live fors." The record says they fought valiantly and defended their faith, religion, country, families, and the honor of their mothers. Of them it was said: "And they were all young men, and they were exceedingly valiant for courage, and also for strength and activity; but behold, this was not all—they were men who were true at all times in whatsoever thing they were entrusted. Yea, they were men of truth and soberness, for they had been taught to keep the commandments of God and to walk uprightly before him."[23]

Jane's Ordeal

I know of a young lady—a modern daughter of Onitah—who had her "die fors" firmly in mind and who would not compromise her standards under very trying circumstances. Jane had gone to a formal dance with a young man she thought she could trust. During the course of the evening, however, her date betrayed her trust by drinking alcoholic beverages and engaging in behavior contrary to her standards and what she had supposed were his also. Despite her pleadings and her appeals to his sense of honor, his demeanor and conduct worsened. When she could see that her safety and perhaps even her virtue was being threatened, she left the dance hall and walked three miles in her formal attire on a snow-packed country road to reach home. Jane barely survived that cold winter evening. However, her "stake" labeled "This I will not do" had been driven deep into her soul and she would not make any concessions.

Preventive Action

How often have we heard the saying "An ounce of prevention is worth a pound of cure"? This is certainly true when it comes to you and the challenges of growing up in righteousness. In addition to deciding early in life your "die fors" before temptation comes you must resolve unequivocally to obey God's commandments. A young man must not surround himself with beer-guzzling and cigarette-smoking companions before deciding whether or not to observe the Word of Wisdom. A young lady must not allow herself to be lured into a friend's apartment before deciding whether or not to live the law of chastity or to safeguard her virtue. It is too late! Too risky! Decisions to refrain from participating in law-breaking behavior must be made well in advance, else peer pressures and circumstances of the moment may prove overpowering.

There is sage counsel in President Kimball's words: "Develop discipline of self so that, more and more, you do not have to decide and redecide what you will do when you are confronted with the same temptation time and time again. You need only to decide some things once. . . . The sooner you take a stand, the taller you will be."[24]

It would be a good thing if you resolved to live according to these simple yet powerfully protective guidelines:

> If it is not *clean*, do not think it.
> If it is not *true*, do not say it.
> If it is not *good*, do not do it.

Seven Enemies of the Soul

A favorite author of mine listed seven enemies of the soul. They are: Sir Pride, Sir Covetousness, Sir Lust, Sir Anger, Sir Gluttony, Sir Envy, and Sir Sloth.[25] All of these demons are the evil companions and squires of that arch-enemy of mankind, Hardness of Heart. Their common cause is to silence and cripple the "inner man" so that the fleshly part of a young man or woman is made to rule over the soul. Each of the seven is a fierce warrior and wields the sword of disobedience. And all of them laugh and rejoice with Satan and his angels[26] when people, especially the young, disobey God's commandments and suffer the consequences.

But there are three champions of the soul who are far more powerful than the seven evil knights mentioned above. I speak of Sir Cleanliness, Sir Truthfulness, and Sir Goodness. These valiant soldiers have "put on the whole armour of God," thus enabling them to overpower and lay low Hardness of Heart and his henchmen. They are always on the side of those who love God and keep his commandments. Do you want spiritual powers on your side? If so, you must be obedient and allow the "inner man" to govern the affairs of your life.[27] Remember: "He that hath no rule over his own spirit is like a city that is broken down and without walls."[28] Furthermore, "He that ruleth his spirit [is mightier] than he that taketh a city."[29]

*   *   *

You might ask, What does God require of me? Does he expect me to place something upon a sacrificial altar, as Abraham did? Does he expect me to build an ark, as Noah did? Does he expect me to seek another land, as Lehi did? Just what does God expect or require of me, anyway?

Ancient Israel was instructed:

> What doth the Lord thy God require of thee, but to fear the Lord thy God, to walk in all his ways, and to love him, and to serve the Lord thy God with all thy heart and with all thy soul,
>
> To keep the commandments of the Lord, and his statutes, which I command thee this day for thy good?[30]

Modern Israel has been told:

> All that [God] requires of you is to keep his commandments; and he has promised you that if you would keep his commandments ye should prosper in the land; and he never doth vary from that which he hath said; therefore, if ye do keep his commandments he doth bless you and prosper you.[31]
>
> Behold, the Lord requireth the heart and a willing mind; and the willing and obedient shall eat the good of the land of Zion in these last days.[32]

You may wonder why the Lord requires of you covenants, commandments, laws, or obligations of any sort. You may say, If he loves us, why does he restrict us? Here is the answer to such a question: "Just as any father would restrict his child, if it is a blessing to that child, so our Father gives us these laws and ordinances and commandments and covenants, not that we should be burdened or restricted by them, but that we may be lifted up and made free, that our burdens may be light; that we may, through obedience to them, more nearly perfect our lives and thereby prepare ourselves for the glories that await those who are willing to conform to the laws and ordinances of the gospel. His laws are not grievous; they are not burdensome."[33]

If you soften your heart and obey God's commandments you will walk a type of escalator on the way to success and happiness. Your personal energies and efforts will be abetted by the unseen but real powers provided by a loving Heavenly Father who is bound to assist the obedient. You will take one step forward and the spiritual belt upon which you are moving will lengthen your stride, quicken your pace, and cushion your feet.

Notes

1. Robert L. Simpson, *Improvement Era*, December 1970, p. 95.
2. Cecil B. DeMille, BYU Commencement Address, May 31, 1957.
3. Deuteronomy 11:26–28.
4. D&C 82:10.
5. Moses 5:6.
6. D&C 89:18–21.
7. Ephesians 6:1–3.
8. D&C 59:15–16.
9. Malachi 3:10–12.
10. Richard L. Evans, *Ensign*, June 1971, p. 74.
11. *For the Strength of Youth*, p. 6.
12. Mary E. Potter, "A Standard of Excellence," *Reader's Digest*, January 1994, pp. 95–96.
13. Zechariah 12:1.
14. See Acts 17:28.
15. See Hebrews 12:9.
16. D&C 88:15.
17. Alma 12:14.
18. Mosiah 4:30.
19. Dean Bruce L. Christensen, BYU, as reported in *Comm World*, no. 30, October 1993.
20. *The Miracle of Forgiveness*, p. 236.
21. Abraham 1:11.
22. See Daniel 1:8–17; 3:13–18.
23. Alma 53:20–21.
24. Spencer W. Kimball, *President Kimball Speaks Out* (Salt Lake City: Deseret Book Co., 1981), p. 94.

25. A. Conan Doyle, *The White Company,* p. 62.
26. See Moses 7:26.
27. See Ephesians 6:11–18.
28. Proverbs 25:28.
29. Proverbs 16:32.
30. Deuteronomy 10:12–13.
31. Mosiah 2:22.
32. D&C 64:34.
33. ElRay L. Christiansen, Conference Report, April 1955, p. 29.

CHAPTER 5

To Avoid Hardness of Heart—
Obey Loving Parents

A story told by President N. Eldon Tanner points to the lifelong benefits of obeying and honoring good parents:

> One of the Ten Commandments states: "Honour thy father and thy mother: that thy days may be long upon the land which the Lord thy God giveth thee" (Exodus 20:12).
>
> A good example of this is found in a little story which I heard recently. A young boy was playing baseball with his friends when his mother's voice came loud and clear, calling, "Charlie, Charlie!" He instantly threw down his bat, picked up his jacket and cap, and started for home.
>
> "Don't go yet; finish the game!" cried the other players.
>
> "I must go right this minute. I told my mother I would come when she called," was Charlie's response.
>
> "Pretend you didn't hear," said the boys.
>
> "But I did hear," said Charlie.
>
> "She won't know you did."
>
> "But I know it, and I've got to go."
>
> One of the boys finally said, "Oh, let him go. You can't change his mind. He's tied to his mother's apron string. He's such a baby he runs the minute she calls."

As he ran off, Charlie called back, "I don't call it babyish to keep one's word to his mother. I call it manly, and the boy who doesn't keep his word to her will never keep it to anyone else."

Years later Charlie became a prosperous businessman and president of a large corporation. His associates always said "His word is his bond," and during a press interview on one occasion he was asked how he acquired such a reputation. His response: "I never broke my word when a boy, no matter how great a temptation, and the habits formed then have clung to me through life."[1]

Why We Should Honor Our Parents

Unfortunately there are a few young people who regard parental counsel as something suspect—even babyish—and who scoff at Charlie and others for honoring their parents. Such scoffers are diagnosed as having a form of hardness of heart which, if not treated, may develop into something life-threatening. Their symptoms are: (1) they fail to realize or have forgotten that the injunction "Honour thy father and thy mother" is one of the Ten Commandments;[2] (2) they do not understand that parents are really agents of God and have been given the awesome responsibility to bring up their children "in the nurture and admonition of the Lord," else they (the parents) will be held accountable;[3] (3) they do not appreciate the fact that most parents attempt to fulfill their heaven-imposed responsibilities in love and with the best interests of the children in mind; (4) they disregard the reality that parents have already walked the slippery path of youth and through their own experiences are now qualified to counsel those who follow them; and (5) they have not kept in mind the promises or blessings associated with the divine decree, "Honour thy father and mother," otherwise there would be no reluctance to obey loving parents in righteousness.

A Commandment with Promise

The commandment to honor parents is found throughout the scriptures. It was given to ancient Israel, reinforced by

Christ and his disciples in New Testament days, and revealed again in modern times. So it isn't necessary to take up space in this discussion with the stating of the same words over and over again. I do, however, feel that it is important to consider statements attached to the commandment by several scriptural writers. Note the statements italicized below:

- "Children, obey your parents in the Lord: *for this is right*."[4]
- "Children, obey your parents in all things: *for this is well pleasing unto the Lord*."[5]
- "For God commanded, saying, Honour thy father and mother: *and, he that curseth father or mother, let him die the death*."[6]
- "Honour thy father and mother; (which is the first commandment with promise;) *that it may be well with thee, and thou mayest live long on the earth*."[7]
- "Honour thy father and thy mother, as the Lord thy God hath commanded thee; *that thy days may be prolonged, and that it may go well with thee, in the land which the Lord thy God giveth thee*."[8]

All of God's commandments are right. They have to be because they come from *the* source of truth and light. Moreover, the Lord, like all fathers, is pleased when his laws are obeyed. As John said: "I have no greater joy than to hear that my children walk in truth."[9] Over the course of time, most parents come to feel the truthfulness of John's remark. But I emphasize the words italicized in the two quotations above that deal with the dual promise: "That thy days may be prolonged, and that it may go well with thee, in the land which the Lord thy God giveth thee."[10]

What youth, whose life is really just beginning, does not want to claim the promise of a long life? What youth does not want to prosper or have things go well with him or her in whatever place or under whatever circumstance? No, there is no specific number of years mentioned, nor is there a definite delineation of how one might prosper by honoring his parents. One may prosper in many ways, and things may go well temporally, spiritually, or both. Still, the promise is given and the word of God is sure, so only the foolish and hard-of-heart youth ignore parental advice when it is given in love and in the spirit of genuine helpfulness.

Wanton Experimentation—A Dangerous Practice

Some young people entertain the fallacious and deadly idea that youth is a time for wanton or unrestrained experimentation. They say to each other, "You only go around once, so you should try everything." Such thinking is very dangerous and can lead to serious problems.

What daughter is so foolish as to place her hand upon the top of a red-hot stove to test the veracity of a mother's warning? What son would drive an automobile into the path of a fast-moving freight train to test the strength of the locomotive, despite the repeated cautions of a concerned father? Young people who play on the hole of the asp usually get bitten. Those who play with wildfire almost always get burned. The sooner youth learn the wisdom of obeying rules, honoring laws, keeping commandments, and following the counsel of loving parents, the happier they will be—to say nothing of the safety they will enjoy.

"I Killed Him"

Two high school friends who hadn't seen each other for many years visited together in a home. Their talk centered upon the choice experiences of yesteryear and the many classmates who were involved. One by one names were mentioned, and story by story cherished memories were shared. What started out as casual conversation soon became more and more personal.

Max asked: "Do you remember Jack?"

"Yes," responded Mike, "I remember him very well, but I haven't seen him since our graduation day."

"Jack died last week," announced Max in an emotion-filled voice. "He became an alcoholic and drank himself into the grave."

Mike expressed his sorrow about the news of Jack's un-
timely death, noticing that tears were welling up in his friend's
eyes.

After a long and awkward silence, Max continued, "Do you
know who introduced Jack to alcohol? Do you know who gave
him his first drink?"

"No, I don't," answered Mike.

"I did," Max confessed. "I enticed him—even dared him to
drink his first bottle of beer. I killed him!"

By this time Max was weeping openly. Mike could see that
his friend was carrying a heavy burden upon his conscience, for
he had assumed personal responsibility for Jack's addiction to a
substance that eventually proved lethal.

Mike made a weak attempt to soothe the injured feelings of
his friend by saying that Jack had his own agency and that he
had probably been influenced by other people. He also placed
his arm around Max's shoulder and expressed his love, knowing that words always seem weak and inadequate when one is
trying to relieve another from self-imposed feelings of guilt.

Max turned the conversation and asked: "Mike, why didn't
you drink with all the others? Everyone but you experimented
and played with the stuff. Why didn't you join the group and
party with Jack, me, and the rest?"

Mike answered simply and honestly, "There are two reasons
why I didn't experiment with alcohol, tobacco, and other habit-
forming substances. First, I didn't take my first drink or smoke
my first cigarette because I wasn't certain whether my first
would be my last. I was afraid I would be starting something I
couldn't stop or give up. I was afraid."

Continued Mike: "It took me years to realize that my built-
in fears of alcohol, tobacco, and the other deadly things were really a blessing from God. Remember the prayer of Nephi, one
of our scriptural heroes? 'O Lord, wilt thou redeem my soul?
Wilt thou deliver me out of the hands of mine enemies? Wilt
thou make me that I may shake at the appearance of sin?' (2
Nephi 4:31.) Oh, how I thank God that I was made to shake at
the appearance of evil!"

Said Mike, "Second, I did not smoke and drink because my
mother and dad not only taught me the difference between

right and wrong but they also taught me this protective truth: 'Watch and pray continually, that ye may not be tempted above that which ye can bear, and thus be led by the Holy Spirit, becoming humble, meek, submissive, patient, full of love and all long-suffering' (Alma 13:28)."

Mike added: "Over the years I have listened to that still small voice within me and I have discovered that it becomes more and more discernible and distinctive as my resolve to resist temptation grows. I have come to regard that voice with its promptings as a type of surrogate mother and father, if you please. Its whisperings have a familiar sound, and, when it speaks to me, I feel as if I am in the presence of my parents receiving loving counsel."

It is a regrettable thing when youth dishonor parents, break rules, and entice others to do the same. Under such circumstances they are made to suffer the scorching pains that result from an earlier hardness of heart, just as Max did. Even worse, they who invite or dare others to engage in sinful practices serve as instruments in the hands of the evil one—Old Scratch, Satan, Lucifer, or call him what you will.

How much better and happier all around it is when youth obey loving parents, heed their counsel and the warnings of the Holy Spirit, and clothe themselves with the protective covering of prayer!

"Walking Bundles of Habits"

At times, young people forget that sin is subtle and vice is vicious. It can begin so innocently, grow so very quietly and quickly, and consume us so completely. What starts as a simple, "I dare you," or as a quiet experiment, can become a binding habit in a short time.

The philosopher and psychologist William James wrote:

> The hell to be endured hereafter, of which theology tells, is no worse than the hell we make for ourselves in this world by habitually fashioning our characters in the wrong way. Could the young but realize how soon they will become

mere walking bundles of habits, they would give more heed to their conduct while in the plastic state. We are spinning our own fates, good or evil, and never to be undone. Every smallest stroke of virtue or of vice leaves its never so little scar. The drunken Rip Van Winkle, in Jefferson's play, excuses himself for every fresh dereliction by saying, "I won't count this time!" Well! he may not count it, and a kind Heaven may not count it; but it is being counted none the less. Down among his nerve-cells and fibres the molecules are counting it, registering and storing it up to be used against him when the next temptation comes. Nothing we ever do is, in strict scientific literalness, wiped out. Of course, this has its good side as well as its bad one. As we become permanent drunkards by so many separate drinks, so we become saints in the moral, and authorities and experts in the practical and scientific spheres, by so many separate acts and hours of work. Let no youth have any anxiety about the upshot of his education, whatever the line of it may be. If he keeps faithfully busy each hour of the working-day, he may safely leave the final result to itself. He can with perfect certainty count on waking up some fine morning, to find himself one of the competent ones of his generation, in whatever pursuit he may have singled out.[11]

James's words remind me of a short and provocative line recorded in the Book of Mormon, which reads: "He [Satan] leadeth them by the neck with a flaxen cord, until he bindeth them with his strong cords forever."[12] The first wrongdoing is like a single strand of flaxen thread; it is easily broken and thrown aside. But each time the wrong is repeated another strand is intertwined around the first, and on and on it goes until an almost unbreakable cord of multi-strands is woven. "The chains of habit," said Samuel Johnson, "are too small to be felt until they are too strong to be broken."

Attentive parents are often the first to see questionable habits forming in the lives of their children. It may be in the way a child walks or talks or eats or dresses or even chooses friends. Whatever it is that seems to be awry in the lives of the children, the parents are derelict in their responsibilities if they do not offer needed advice or corrections, and the children will come up wanting if they do not accept it in good faith. No parent sits idly and watches a thug bind up a child with strong cords and carry him away for some questionable purpose. Similarly, no caring parent will remain silent or stand aside while a child slowly succumbs to a destructive habit or influence. It is therefore quite essential that you, while in your plastic state, curb your own desires and obey your parents. You must not regard parents as old-fashioned or artifacts of the past. Rather, you must respect them as more experienced "stand-ins" for the Lord who know what is best for their children over the long haul.

Parents and Chastening

Paul, the ancient apostle, reminds us of this exhortation: "My son, despise not thou the chastening of the Lord, nor faint when thou art rebuked of him: for whom the Lord loveth he chasteneth." He adds: "No chastening for the present seemeth to be joyous, but grievous: nevertheless afterward it yieldeth the peaceable fruit of righteousness unto them which are exercised thereby."[13]

Parents, like the Lord, love their children. Therefore they chasten their sons and daughters when they are in need of correction. This is not done because it brings Mother and Dad pleasure, but because they want to spare their young ones unnecessary suffering and sorrow. Few parents enjoy "reproving betimes with sharpness, when moved upon by the Holy Ghost."[14] But they would rather chastise now than weep later with children who have made serious mistakes—mistakes that might have been avoided if frank counsel had been given earlier.

"Furthermore," wrote Paul, "we have had fathers of our flesh which corrected us, and we gave them reverence: shall we not much rather be in subjection unto the Father of spirits, and live?"[15] These words make it abundantly clear that you should honor and "be in subjection" to the will of your Heavenly Father and honor your earthly father and give him reverence, even though he corrects and chastises you on occasions.

Marci's Proposal

Marci reverenced her parents. That is why she sought their counsel soon after she had received a marriage proposal from a young man. The two had dated at college for several months and they seemed to have much in common. Both were religious; both loved children; and both loved the Lord. Her suitor had professed his love and good intentions. Marci wasn't so sure.

Mother and Dad were not able at the time to visit Marci at school, where the proposal could have been discussed at length. But they promised to fast and pray over the matter before sharing their advice. Their love for Marci was deep and abiding. No parents had ever raised a more obedient daughter than she.

A few days later, Marci's parents called her back on the telephone. Their response was simply: "We have prayed and pondered over your proposal and we don't have a good feeling. We cannot tell you why these feelings have been so negative. Moreover, we are reluctant to judge the young man because we have never met him. But we don't think that you should accept the engagement ring."

Though temporarily disappointed with the response from her mother and father, Marci trusted their feelings and accepted their counsel without argument and ended the courtship. There was no debate, no crying, and no appeal for additional consideration. She trusted implicitly in her parents' word, knowing that it had been spoken in love and out of the deepest concern for her well-being.

Later, Marci's father wrote:

> Marci, I remind you that you are a very special young lady. Your body is clean, your mind pure, and your spirit strong. Therefore, be very cautious in all your dealings. Don't permit anyone to stain your soul or mar your character. Although at times you may get lonely or wonder if that knight in shining armor will ever arrive, I assure you that he will in due time. Consider it this way: The reason he (the knight) is taking so long is that he is strengthening and polishing his armor. When it is sufficiently prepared, he will

come and claim you his. You see, this added time of waiting is given to you and him as a time of preparation. Consequently, both of you will be far better equipped to fight the battles of life and to protect the children that will bless your relationship.

Just be patient, prayerful and clean. Trust the Lord and he will extend his blessings in due time. We love you, dear. Our hopes, wishes, and desires are only for your eternal happiness. God bless you always.[16]

A few months later "Mr. Right" came upon the scene. He took Marci to the temple, where they were sealed together for time and for all eternity. In the years that have followed, Marci has testified concerning this important, scripture-based fact: Loving parents do not chasten or give advice after their own pleasures; they do it for the profit of the children so that the children might be partakers of holiness and happiness.[17]

We All Make Mistakes

President Ezra Taft Benson made this profound statement:

Our parents deserve our honor and respect for giving us life itself. Beyond this they almost always made countless sacrifices as they cared for and nurtured us through our infancy and childhood, provided us with the necessities of life, and nursed us through physical illnesses and the emotional stresses of growing up. In many instances, they provided us with the opportunity to receive an education, and, in a measure, they educated us. Much of what we know and do we learned from their example. May we ever be grateful to them and show that gratitude.

Let us also learn to be forgiving of our parents, who, perhaps having made mistakes as they reared us, almost always did the best they knew how. May we ever forgive them as we would likewise wish to be forgiven by our own children for mistakes we make.[18]

In a moment of weakness Lehi, the father of Nephi, murmured against the Lord. It revealed a weakness in Lehi that perhaps Nephi had not seen before. This murmuring must have disappointed Nephi very much. Nevertheless, when needed direction was required soon thereafter, the son honored his father's position by asking, "Whither shall I go to obtain food?"[19]

I'm convinced that special blessings await the youth who reverence their parents through the good times and the bad times—when honest mistakes are made and when the wise suggestions prove to be right. Most of us, like Nephi, were born of "goodly parents,"[20] and the best we can offer in return is to strive to be goodly children.

*   *   *

At the beginning of this chapter, an incident in the life of a young man named Charlie was related. You may recall that despite peer pressure, Charlie kept his word to his mother and obeyed her call to come home. In doing so he may have lost a turn at bat in a sandlot baseball game, but he won the honor of his parents and a lifetime reputation that "his word is his bond." Charlie and others of the same inclination find that obeying loving parents and living the commandments of God are one and the same.

No finer or more appropriate conclusion to this discussion could be given than these words by President Kimball: "If we truly honor [our parents], we will seek to emulate their best characteristics and to fulfill their highest aspirations for us. No gift purchased from a store can begin to match in value to parents some simple, sincere words of appreciation. Nothing we could give them would be more prized than righteous living for each youngster."[21]

Avoid hardness of heart by obeying "your parents in the Lord: for this is right. Honour thy father and mother; (which is the first commandment with promise;) that it may be well with thee, and thou mayest live long on the earth."[22]

Notes

1. As told by N. Eldon Tanner, *Ensign*, November 1977, pp. 43–44; adapted from "True and Faithful," in *Moral Stories for Little Folks* (Salt Lake City: Juvenile Instructor Office, 1891), p. 122.

2. Exodus 20:12.

3. Ephesians 6:4.

4. Ephesians 6:1.

5. Colossians 3:20.

6. Matthew 15:4.

7. Ephesians 6:2–3.

8. Deuteronomy 5:16.

9. 3 John 1:4.

10. Deuteronomy 5:16.

11. William James, *The Principles of Psychology*, 2 vols. (New York: Dover Publications, 1950), 1:127.

12. 2 Nephi 26:22.

13. Hebrews 12:5, 6, 11.

14. D&C 121:43.

15. Hebrews 12:9.

16. Excerpt from a letter written November 2, 1973, by Carlos E. Asay to his daughter Marcianne.

17. See Hebrews 12:10.

18. Ezra Taft Benson, *Ensign*, November 1989, pp. 6–7.

19. 1 Nephi 16:20, 23.

20. 1 Nephi 1:1.

21. *The Teachings of Spencer W. Kimball*, p. 348.

22. Ephesians 6:1–3.

CHAPTER 6

To Avoid Hardness of Heart— *Obey the Eternal Rhythm of Life*

*A*n author looks back on a childhood experience that taught him the wisdom of patiently conforming to nature's patterns and seasons:

> I remembered one morning when I discovered a cocoon in the bark of a tree, just as the butterfly was making a hole in its case and preparing to come out. I waited a while, but it was too long appearing and I was impatient. I bent over it and breathed on it to warm it. I warmed it as quickly as I could and the miracle began to happen before my eyes, faster than life. The case opened, the butterfly started slowly crawling out and I shall never forget my horror when I saw how its wings were folded back and crumpled; the wretched butterfly tried with its whole trembling body to unfold them. Bending over it, I tried to help it with my breath. In vain. It needed to be hatched out patiently and the unfolding of the wings should be a gradual process in the sun. Now it was too late. My breath had forced the butterfly to appear,

all crumpled, before its time. It struggled desperately and, a few seconds later, died in the palm of my hand.

That little body is, I do believe, the greatest weight I have on my conscience. For I realize today that it is a mortal sin to violate the great laws of nature. We should not hurry, we should not be impatient, but we should confidently obey the eternal rhythm.[1]

Sally's Sad Experience

Sally was a beautiful, precocious girl who wanted to grow up too fast. At the ripe old age of fifteen she prevailed upon her parents to allow her to date. Her parents really did not like the idea, but Sally wearied them with her pleadings and they reluctantly gave their consent.

The first few dates included other young couples. Soon, however, group dating ceased and Sally and her partner went to shows, dances, and other places by themselves. More and more time was spent in secluded settings, and step by step the physical contacts increased. What started out as harmless hand-holding grew steadily into something very intimate and very serious.

Early in her sixteenth year, Sally became pregnant. Though her boyfriend was not much older than she and still attending high school, it was decided that they would be married. A wedding ceremony was held in the privacy of the home in which Sally had been reared, and the two immature youths began their marriage.

Both Sally and her husband became school dropouts, for she was with child and he had to scramble for a job. Even before the baby was born the couple began to argue over their forced circumstances. Both yearned for the companionships of friends in school; both missed the church and school activities being enjoyed by peers; both resented the restrictions and responsibilities of married life; and both felt uneasy about their dependency upon Sally's parents for a place to live, the payment of medical bills, and other necessities. Each began to blame the other for all that had happened causing them to enter the adult arena before either was prepared.

When the baby came, things settled down for a few weeks. The young couple loved their daughter and delighted in being parents, although they had to rely upon others for the care of the child. But in due time the novelty of having a baby wore out and the heavy responsibilities of a family became a reality, especially to Sally's husband. He worried about supporting a wife and child—he wasn't certain that he could do it. And he wondered whether this new role as husband and father was really one he wanted to assume.

Soon after her seventeenth birthday the inevitable happened. Sally's husband asked for a divorce, saying that he really didn't love her and that married life was not for him—at least not for now.

So at the ripe old age of seventeen, Sally's life came apart. Here she was a mother, a divorcée, a school dropout, a burden to her parents, and still not even old enough to vote. She had few skills and no training; yet she was faced with the prospects of finding a way to support herself and daughter. She longed for the more carefree days of yesterday while overwhelmed by the responsibilities of today and tomorrow. Deep down within her heart she wished she had been more discreet in her relationship with the opposite sex and more patient in growing up. She wished she had been less hard of heart and more susceptible to the counsel given by loved ones.

"To Every Thing There Is a Season"

Sally's sad experience helps to verify the wisdom found in the words of the Preacher, who said: "To every thing there is a season, and a time to every purpose under the heaven."[2] Yes, there is a time to be born, a time to be a child, a time to be a youth, a time to be an adult, and even a time to die. Each season and time has its purpose and each is a part of the eternal rhythm of life.

Those who believe that God has "made every thing beautiful in his time"[3] will respect the eternal rhythm and take matters in proper sequence, knowing that if they do so they can claim all the blessings life can give.

Speaking to young men, President Kimball counselled: "One

can have all the blessings if he is in control and takes the experiences in proper turn; first some limited social get-acquainted contacts, then his [full-time] mission, then his courting, then his temple marriage and his schooling and his family, then his life's work. In any other sequence he could run into difficulty."[4]

The very same can be said of young women. They too can enjoy a fulness of life and reap a basketful of blessings if they take experiences in proper turn—first some limited social get-acquainted contacts, an education, temple endowment, temple marriage, and a family. There was no sin in Sally's desire for marriage and a family. All young women should keep themselves pointed for marriage and hope to bear children at the appropriate time. However, when they confuse infatuation with love and stumble and fall into the role of a mother before they come of age, before they have acquired homemaking skills, and before they have matured, there will always be disappointments and heartaches.

Said Camilla Kimball: "I would hope that every girl and woman . . . has the desire and ambition to qualify in two vocations—that of homemaking, and that of preparing to earn a living outside the home, if and when the occasion requires."[5] Such qualification and preparation is best accomplished when young women abide the eternal rhythm of life, listen to counsel given by loving parents, and exercise a little patience.

I saw an interesting banner displayed at an Explorer conference being held on a college campus. It read: "Don't wait to be a great man—be a great boy!" Those who posted the banner were not suggesting that goal setting and planning for the future were inappropriate activities for youth. Nor were they implying that boys should not grow up and eventually accept adult responsibilities. They were, however, trying to convince young people that the seeds of greatness are sown in childhood, sprout during adolescence, and find fruition in adulthood. As one writer put it, "Men and women are what happened to little boys and girls."[6]

Lessons of Patience and Waiting

Patience is not a character trait that we normally associate with youth. When most young people want something they want it right now, not tomorrow or the next day. It is difficult for them to wait patiently for something to develop, to hatch out, or to abide its time. They like to see events unfold at a fast pace, in rapid succession, rather than in the more deliberate rhythm of a "waltz." Too many, therefore, attempt to force issues and situations in ways that damage their lives. If only the impatient youth would understand the wisdom found in these lines by President Joseph F. Smith: "Everywhere in nature we are taught the lessons of patience and waiting. We want things a long time before we get them, and the fact that we wanted them a long time makes them all the more precious when they come. In nature we have our seed-time and harvest; and if children were taught that the desires that they sow may be reaped by and by through patience and labor, they will learn to appreciate whenever a long-looked-for goal has been reached. Nature resists us and keeps admonishing us to wait; indeed, we are compelled to wait."[7]

Speaking to the subject of "A Law of Increasing Returns," Elder Henry B. Eyring said: "You rarely can have a photograph of that future for which you now sacrifice, but you can get pictures. Years ago, . . . it occurred to me that I would sometime perhaps have a family. I even joked about them, calling them 'the red heads.' My mother's hair had been red when she was young. I certainly didn't think the idea of red heads was inspiration, just an idea. But more than once that picture was enough to make me work and wait."[8]

You too can reap the blessings of the "Law of Increasing Returns" if you follow the advice given and do three things: (1) Visualize the future as vividly as possible (this goes along with goal setting), (2) work hard and succeed in today's tasks, and (3) wait patiently, not idly, having perfect faith and confidence in what your earnest effort will bring tomorrow.

A Bridge Called Adolescence

It is recorded: "When I was a child, I spake as a child, I understood as a child, I thought as a child: but when I *became* a man, I put away childish things."[9] I emphasize the word *became* because it suggests a time of growth and development—a time when childish things are discarded. A child does not leap suddenly from a state of immaturity to a state of maturity. He or she must walk that bridge which spans the distance between puberty and adulthood. And that bridge is a period of time called adolescence.

Sally had taken only a few faltering steps on the bridge of adolescence when she thought she had arrived on the other side. Consequently she entered the world of the adults before her time, when her "wings were folded back and crumpled." Had she exercised patience and allowed herself time to cross the bridge so that physical, spiritual, mental, and social maturation could have occurred, the outcome would have been much different.

It should be remembered that the only perfect man who ever lived on this earth confidently obeyed the eternal rhythm and walked the bridge of adolescence. The scriptures say little about Christ's childhood and days as a youth. Brief references are made to his circumcision and to the teaching of the doctors in the temple when twelve years of age. But two enlightening verses in Luke provide us with precious information about his maturation process. One verse reads: "And the child grew and waxed strong in spirit, filled with wisdom: and the grace of God was upon him."[10] The other states: "And Jesus increased in wisdom and stature, and in favour with God and man."[11] No, Jesus did not jump impulsively into the adult world, as did Sally. He grew and developed and became a man before he launched into his divine ministry. He walked the bridge of adolescence; he confidently obeyed the eternal rhythm of life. So should all young people.

* * *

There is an orderly sequence of events in this life that must not be offended. The Preacher was right when he declared: "To every thing there is a season, and a time to every purpose under the heaven." And, I would emphasize, a time to be a child, a time to be a youth, and a time to be an adult.

Life does have its seasons, and each season has its own

special experiences and joys, if taken in proper sequence. Therefore those who resist hardness of heart, maintain control of their lives, demonstrate patience, and obey the eternal rhythm can reap all the blessings related to the spring, summer, fall, and winter of living. As Richard L. Evans stated: "The laws of nature, the laws of God, the laws of life, are one and the same and are always in full force. We live in a universe of law. Spring follows winter. This we can count on. The sun will show itself on time again tomorrow morning. This we can count on."[12]

Notes

1. Nikos Kazantzakis, *Zorba the Greek* (New York: Simon and Schuster, 1966), pp. 120–21.

2. Ecclesiastes 3:1.

3. Ecclesiastes 3:11.

4. Spencer W. Kimball, *Ensign,* February 1975, p. 4.

5. Camilla Kimball, *Ensign,* March 1977, p. 59.

6. *Richard Evans' Quote Book* (Salt Lake City: Publishers Press, 1971), p. 32.

7. Joseph F. Smith, *Gospel Doctrine* (Salt Lake City: Deseret Book Co., 1966), p. 298.

8. *Brigham Young University 1981–82 Fireside and Devotional Speeches* (Provo, Utah: University Publications, 1982), p. 125.

9. 1 Corinthians 13:11; emphasis added.

10. Luke 2:40.

11. Luke 2:52.

12. Richard L. Evans, *Ensign,* June 1971, p. 73.

PART III

Pay Close Attention to the Road Signs Posted

*T*ravel on an unposted highway can be very dangerous. Without *caution* signs, motorists may encounter road conditions such as rock slides, loose gravel, or other hazards that are threatening to both themselves and their vehicles. Unless *regulatory* signs are used, movement becomes chaotic, because control instructions, like speed limits and directional procedures, are missing. Similarly, when *yield* signs are not in place, driver courtesy is cast aside and accidents occur.

It is much the same with the young ones who walk the slippery path of youth. Their travel also becomes hazardous if helpful road signs are not posted and heeded. I therefore post three signs in this book: one is a caution to young people, especially the young women, on the subject, "Lust Is Not Love." The second is a regulatory message or a charge addressed to young men pertaining to "Keep Right: Be Men of God." (This charge is equally applicable to young women.) The third sign is a yield sign—one inviting all youth to yield "to the enticings of the Holy Spirit"[1] and to reach desired destinations by becoming all that they should become.

We have all heard the expression, "He who chooses the beginning of a road also chooses its destination." This is a fact, providing the traveller reads the road signs posted along the way and avoids detours, dead-ends, no-parking spaces, and other disruptive influences like blindness of mind and hardness of heart. No road that diverges in a wood, even the one less traveled by,[2] will make much of a difference in your life unless it is that strait and narrow path designated by the master mapmaker, even Jesus of Nazareth.

Notes

1. Mosiah 3:19.
2. See Robert Frost, "The Road Not Taken," in *Poems That Live Forever* (New York: Doubleday, 1955), p. 317.

CHAPTER 7

A Word of Caution to Young Women
Lust Is Not Love

One of the most used and abused words in the English language is the word *love*. It is spoken glibly by people in various settings, making it a well-worn cliché. Movie stars speak the word casually in passionate scenes. Television performers do the same as they attempt to swallow each other with sensual kisses. And many, too many, male predators idly mouth the word as they seek to rob women of their most priceless possession—their virtue.

Lucifer and his cohorts Blindness of Mind and Hardness of Heart have perverted love just as they have other godly characteristics and virtues. In the name of love they encourage illicit sex, ridicule the ordinance of marriage, and scoff at the institution of families. The manner in which they twist and misuse the word *love* reminds me of this warning: "Woe unto them that call evil good, and good evil; that put darkness for light, and light for darkness; that put bitter for sweet, and sweet for bitter!"[1] And, I might add, "woe unto those who call lust love, and love lust."

Although this word of warning is addressed specifically to young women, it also applies to young men. Young men are invited to read these pages, realizing that they too must not confuse lust with love.

105

A Comparison

Perhaps the best way of distinguishing love from lust is to compare the two words as follows:

Lust	Love
Lust is of the flesh and of the world.[2]	Love is a fruit of the Spirit and a godly virtue.[3]
Lust is excessive and uncontrolled sexual desire.	Love is a controlled expression of sexual desire.
Lust is centered in unrestrained self-gratification.	Love is centered in a concern for the welfare and well-being of someone else.
Lust is pleasure-seeking without limits.	Love is joy-seeking within proper bounds and limits.
Lust is a transient expression of feelings.	Love is an enduring expression of feelings with growing respect for another.
Lust leads to actions that are followed by lingering misgivings and regrets.	Love leads to actions that bring peace of conscience and sweet memories.

There are times when a young man may say to a young lady, "If you truly love me, you will. . . ." Or he may challenge a girl's confession of love in this way: "You say you love me, so why don't you prove your words by. . . ." Such words are spoken by selfish, pleasure-seeking, lustful young men. One who really loves a young lady would never suggest "Just this once," nor would he ask her to compromise her standards or surrender her precious virtue with taunting lines like, "Everybody else does it." If he truly loved her he would control his fleshly desires and do all within his power to preserve her "tender and chaste and delicate" status, which status "is pleasing unto God."[4]

Love and Sex

As mentioned above, "Lust is excessive and uncontrolled sexual desire"; whereas, "Love is a controlled expression of sexual desire" and more. It isn't that sex is inherently evil, for it is not. But when it is allowed to run wild something good and of God is perverted. I say this because sex fulfills at least three righteous purposes when expressed within the bonds of marriage and in a caring manner. Those purposes are: (1) procreation (to bring children into existence), (2) the sharing of divine love, and (3) the binding of a husband to a wife and vice versa.

President Gordon B. Hinckley spoke to youth of a voice pleading for virtue and the abstinence from that which is evil. Said he:

> You should recognize, you must recognize, that both experience and divine wisdom dictate virtue and moral cleanliness as the way that leads to strength of character, peace in the heart, and happiness in life. Will and Ariel Durant, who wrote eleven large volumes of history covering thousands of years, declared: "A youth boiling with hormones will wonder why he should not give full freedom to his sexual desires; and if he is unchecked by customs, morals, or laws, he may ruin his life before he matures sufficiently to understand that sex is a river of fire that must be banked and cooled by a hundred restraints if it is not to consume in chaos both the individual and the group."

President Hinckley added: "For your own sakes, for your happiness now and in all the years to come, and for the happiness of the generations who come after you, avoid sexual transgression as you would a plague."[5]

I remember an experience of years ago that taught me a powerful lesson about love and sex. It occurred when I was in high school and involved a well-respected priesthood leader who married in his mid-twenties, after having served a full-time mission and completing some military service. Upon his return from the honeymoon, a group of my associates crowded about the newlywed and asked with a carnal ring in their voices, "Well,_____, how is married life?" The question was not only an intrusion upon his private life but also one that fished for a sexy response.

The young leader squared his shoulders, looked us straight in the eyes, and answered reverently, "If God had anything better, he must have kept it for himself." He then proceeded to instruct us concerning the sacredness of sex and the beauty of marriage. It was a lesson I shall never forget.

Be it ever understood: "That passion which produces petting and other immorality is a prostitution of love. There are counterfeit leaden dollars, counterfeit greenbacks, not worth a dime a ton. There are spurious concepts and ideologies. Love has its counterfeit: lust, which is mistaken by the unsuspecting as genuine."[6]

Tests of Love

Though love is something that cannot be weighed on a scale or measured by a tape, it is something that can be tested.

Elder John A. Widtsoe offered four tests by which love might be recognized. Those tests are reported below with my brief comments:

1. "Love is always founded in truth." It is free of lies or any form of deceit. One who falsifies to a loved one or God does not really possess the virtue of love.

2. "Love does not offend or hurt or injure the loved one." Any form of cruelty, whether mentally or physically imposed, betrays expressions of love. Any form of abuse is the antithesis of love. So called "tough love" is an oxymoron—the two words are contradictory and do not belong together.[7]

3. "Love is a positive active force. . . . If there is need, love tries to supply it. If there is weakness, love supplants it with strength. . . . Love that does not help is a faked or transient love."

4. "True love sacrifices for the loved one." Such true love is modeled by a mother who jeopardizes her very life for a child, a father who gives a kidney to a son dying of nephritis, and a young couple who delays marriage to serve a mission.[8]

Regardless of what the voices of the world say about love, true love includes the elements of truth, kindness, support, and sacrifice. It was so in the beginning, it is the same today, and it will remain so forever, because love is an eternal virtue and is as unchangeable as God himself.

Am I in Love?

In answer to the question, "How may I know when I am in love?" President David O. McKay quoted a friend as saying: "My mother once said that if you meet a girl in whose presence you feel a desire to achieve, who inspires you to do your best, and to make the most of yourself, such a young woman is worthy of your love and is awakening love in your heart." President McKay added: "I submit that as a true guide. In the presence of the girl you truly love you do not feel to grovel; in her presence you do not attempt to take advantage of her; in her presence you feel that you would like to be everything that a 'Master Man' should become, for she will inspire you to that ideal."[9]

I used this "true guide" of President McKay's on one occasion when I was counselling a young lady. This particular coed, a beauty queen, rose to the head of my class at the beginning of a semester and toward the middle came dangerously close to failing. I met with her and asked why her performance in class had dropped so suddenly. She guessed that her problem was related to her courtship—a courtship that seemed directed toward marriage.

I had an uneasy feeling about my student's situation, so I asked: "Do you really love the young man you are dating, and does he really love you?" After a short pause, she replied, "I think so." I wondered if she had heard of President McKay's "goodness test" of love. She had not. I therefore applied it by asking some questions.

"What has happened to your studies since you began dating seriously?"

"I'm failing all of my classes," she admitted.

I said, "Is that good?"

"No," she confessed, "that isn't so good."

"What has happened to your church attendance and activity in recent weeks?"

"My boyfriend isn't all that religious. We often skip church on Sunday."

"Is that good?"

"No, that isn't good."

"Final question," I added. "What has happened to your relationships with roommates and family members of late?"

She lowered her head and said: "My boyfriend is very jealous of my time and tries to monopolize my life. As a result of this, I am not as close to my friends and family as I should be."

"Is that good?"

"No," she said once more, "that is not good."

"My dear," I concluded, "I do not need to ask any more questions. Your intended has failed miserably the goodness test of love. Do be careful. Don't make a mistake that may blight your life eternally."

It was obvious to me that the young man's professed love was mocked by his actions. His influence upon the girl was not positive or building; nor did it suggest that he was making any sacrifice in her behalf. What he was doing to her was actually cruel, selfish, and abusive. His was a pseudo-love.

The young lady left my office with tears in her eyes, making me wonder if my advice had been too blunt. A few days later, however, she came bounding into my classroom with renewed spirit and a smile on her face and announced, "I gave him the boot and I haven't felt this good in a long time."

You must be very, very careful. Do not confuse "passing fancies" or fleeting physical attractions with true love. Otherwise, you may make serious mistakes and reap years and years of hardship and heartache.

I like President Kimball's succinct statement: "To love is to *give*, not to take. To love is to *serve*, not to exploit."[10]

A heartfelt confession of love has its place; but if that confession of love is not supported by acts of giving, serving, and obeying, it is as "sounding brass, or a tinkling cymbal."[11]

True Love—A Triangular Arrangement

True or abiding love may be illustrated as a triangle, as shown in the accompanying diagram.

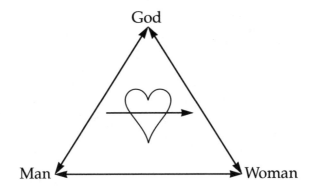

In this arrangement, the man looks to a woman and is more concerned about her life than he is his own. The woman has eyes only for the man and places his welfare beyond that of her own. Both the man and the woman look to God, knowing that he will sanction and bless their love so long as they live righteously.

While it is true that the seeds of love may be planted with physical attraction, true love sprouts and grows as the spiritual attractions or inner feelings become more and more predominant. This is why true love is referred to as being more than skin deep. This is why true love grows over the years in an honorable companionship, even though age takes its toll on the physical body. This is why true love is three-dimensional in nature. And this is why true love increases during times of adversity, illness, and other difficulties.

Perhaps these words of President Kimball's will provide you with a better mental image of this true love triangle: "You must forget yourself and love your companion more than yourself. . . . If two people love the Lord more than their own lives and then love each other more than their own lives, working together in total harmony with the gospel program . . . they are sure to have this great happiness."[12]

* * *

"Love," said the Prophet Joseph Smith, "is one of the chief characteristics of Deity, and ought to be manifested by those who aspire to be the sons [and daughters] of God."[13] It is one of those virtues we must acquire if we expect to become saints through the atonement of Christ.[14] Moreover, it is the core of all the teachings of Jesus Christ during his ministry on earth. No one of us will ever stand in the Lord's presence with clear conscience or ever hope to become even as he is unless he or she understands love, acquires it, and expresses it properly to others.

I warn you, then, that lust is not love. Do not believe what carnal, conniving, and hard-hearted people are saying. Rather, settle only for that three-dimensional love which is enduring, edifying, and fully acceptable to you, to the object of your affections, and to God.

Notes

1. Isaiah 5:20.
2. 1 John 2:16.
3. Galatians 5:22.
4. Jacob 2:7.
5. Gordon B. Hinckley, *Ensign*, May 1987, p. 48.
6. Spencer W. Kimball, Conference Report, Sydney Australia Area Conference, 1976, p. 54.
7. See D&C 121:4–46.
8. John A. Widtsoe, *An Understandable Religion* (Salt Lake City: Deseret Book Co., 1944), pp. 72–73.
9. David O. McKay, *Gospel Ideals* (Salt Lake City: *Improvement Era*, 1953), p. 459.
10. *Faith Precedes the Miracle* (Salt Lake City: Deseret Book Co., 1972), p. 157.
11. 1 Corinthians 13:1.
12. Spencer W. Kimball, *Marriage* (Salt Lake City, Deseret Book Co., 1978), pp. 10, 49.
13. *Teachings of the Prophet Joseph Smith*, Joseph Fielding Smith, comp. (Salt Lake City: Deseret Book Co., 1971), p. 174.
14. See Mosiah 3:19.

CHAPTER 8

A Charge to Young Men
Keep Right—
Be Men of God

*A*n adolescent young man reported: "I feel a lot of pressure from my friends to smoke and steal and things like that. . . . My best friends are really pushing me to [smoke]. They call me a pansy and a momma's boy if I don't. I really don't like the idea of smoking but my good friend Steve told me in front of some of our friends, 'Kevin, you're an idiot and a chicken wrapped up in one little body.'"[1]

An eighteen-year-old recounted:

> On one occasion, I was persuaded to join a group on a weekend excursion. I was told that the [plans] for the day included . . . sightseeing, a lunch, and a movie. I was promised that there would be no [inappropriate activities].

Although this chapter is addressed specifically to young men, it also has application to young women. Young women are invited to read these pages with these words in mind: "Be Women of God."

All . . . knew that I was a Latter-day Saint and . . . deeply committed to the moral standards of the Church.

Upon reaching the city, we visited a place or two of historical significance and ate lunch. Then the inevitable happened—the group turned toward a bar and a house of [prostitution]. I refused to enter these dens of iniquity, and I openly expressed my anger over the broken promises of my associates.

As I walked away . . . my companions taunted me by shouting, "When are you going to grow up?" "When are you going to be a man?"[2]

Who Is a Man?

It seems that everyone at some time or another is invited by peers to smoke, drink, steal, or engage in other immoral acts, all under the pretense of manhood. And when someone refuses to participate, he is often ridiculed and called names like pansy, momma's boy, idiot, chicken, sissy, and religious fanatic. Such names are used by peers who equate manliness with the ability to drink liquor, blow tobacco smoke out of all the facial cavities, sow one's wild oats like some animal on the street, and break moral laws without a twinge of conscience.

We see colorful advertisements on billboards, in magazines, and on the television screen promoting cigarettes, beer, and other vices. Those who use cunning tactics to peddle their wares disregard the souls of young people and love only their money. They would have us believe that a person with a cigarette or alcoholic beverage in hand is a man, when in reality he is nothing more than a slave to a destructive substance. They would have us believe that a person who engages in illicit sex is a man, when in reality he is nothing more than an abuser of those who are meant to be "tender," "chaste," and "delicate."[3] They would have us believe that brute force or crude behavior, uncontrolled temper, foul language, and dirty appearance make a man, when in reality these characteristics are animalistic at best and the opposite of manhood at worst.

You must be on guard; you must not be influenced by barbarian voices in your quest to become a man.[4] You must remember that "God created man in his own image" and that man is expected to keep that image engraven upon his countenance.[5]

"What is man?" asked the psalmist. The answer: "[God] made him a little lower than the angels, and hast crowned him with glory and honour."[6] It is therefore your responsibility to climb ever upward and to wear God-given crowns honorably. Young men, especially those of a "chosen generation" and "royal priesthood," must understand that they are the spiritual offspring of God and that no one becomes in truth a man until he reverences the Father of spirits and allows inner powers to control his thoughts, words, and actions.[7]

What Makes a Man a Man?

"What makes a man a man?" This is a question used in a popular beer ad. The suggestion of that advertisement is that by drinking the beer the consumer becomes a man. How devious the approach and how very stupid the concept! Those who try to get you to drink alcoholic beverages and use drugs have total disregard for you, you who are the "temples of God." Hence they would have you defile your body and offend the Spirit of God that dwells within you.[8]

What makes a man a man? Let's turn to the Book of Mormon and father Lehi for an answer. A short time before his death, Lehi gave this charge to his rebellious sons: "Arise from the dust, . . . and be men."[9]

Awake from a deep sleep, yea, even from the sleep of hell, and shake off the awful chains by which ye are bound.[10]

Be determined in one mind and in one heart, united in all things.[11]

Put on the armor of righteousness. . . . Come forth out of obscurity. . . . Rebel no more.[12]

The challenge to "arise from the dust" means to overcome evil behaviors that destroy character and ruin lives. Physical appetites must be controlled.

"Awake from a deep sleep . . . even from the sleep of hell" suggests a process of learning and becoming aware of God's holy purposes. No sleep is deeper or more deadly than the sleep of ignorance.

"Shake off the awful chains by which ye are bound" indicates the need to overcome bad habits, even the seemingly little habits that grow into strong "chains of hell."[13]

"Be determined in one mind and in one heart, united in all things" requires full commitment to righteousness and a singleness of purpose so that one's will is made compatible with the will of God.

"Put on the armor of righteousness" reminds us of the need to wear the helmet of salvation, pick up the sword of truth, use the shield of faith, and accept the full protective coverings of the Lord.[14]

"Come forth out of obscurity" instructs us to model goodness and serve as a light to others. True men are living light fountains which are pleasant to be near.[15]

"Rebel no more" makes it perfectly clear that ignoring or willfully breaking commandments is a wasteful effort.

You Can't Be Too Righteous

There is a dangerous error circulating among some Latter-day Saints and taking its toll among the young. It is that a "balanced man" is one who deliberately guards against becoming too righteous. This misconception would have you believe that it is possible to live successfully and happily as a "double-minded man,"[16] that is, with one foot in Babylon and one foot in Zion.

I love the story of two young men who had been schooled in a monastery. One morning as they sought adventure, they passed a cathedral. The more righteous of the two remembered that they had not prayed that morning and said, "How can [we] hope for [God's] blessing upon the day?"

The less righteous one responded: "My friend, I have prayed so much during the last two months . . . that I feel that I have [somewhat] over-prayed myself."

"How can a man have too much religion?" asked the first. "It is the one thing that availeth. A man is but a beast as he lives from day to day, eating and drinking, breathing and sleeping. It is only when he raises himself, and concerns himself with the immortal spirit within him, that he becomes in very truth a man. Bethink ye how sad a thing it would be that the blood of the Redeemer should be spilled to no purpose."[17]

Can a person be too righteous? Too Christlike? Impossible! Can the so-called "balanced man" walk successfully the beam between good and evil? No. Each step is shaky, and eventually he will teeter and fall and break himself against the commandments of God.

Fleshliness never was manliness, and it never will be. A real man is one who yields to the enticings of the Holy Spirit and seeks to acquire Christlike virtues. A real man is one who allows the Spirit to direct the course and to call the cadence in his life. "Remember, to be carnally-minded is death, and to be spiritually-minded is life eternal."[18]

Examples of Manliness

On October 1, 1959, a man of Christ stood before a crowd of fifteen hundred people in a church within the shadow of the Kremlin and boldly referred to Jesus as the great Redeemer. Here are some of his words, which were spoken in an emotion-filled voice: "I believe very firmly in prayer. I know it is possible to reach out and tap that Unseen Power which gives us strength and such an anchor in time of need. . . . Be unafraid, keep His commandments, love one another, pray for peace and all will be well. . . . Truth will endure. Time is on the side of truth."[19]

People wept openly on that occasion, including United States newsmen who had reluctantly attended the worship service. One newsman, a former marine, ranked the experience as one of the two most spiritual and memorable of his life.

There was a man in that cathedral in Russia on that special day. His name, Ezra Taft Benson—who would become the thirteenth President and prophet of the Church.

Parley P. Pratt provides us with a description of a real man in his account of his imprisonment in Richmond, Missouri, with Joseph Smith and others. On one of those awful nights in jail, Elder Pratt and his associates were exposed to the filthy language of their guards as they bragged of their deeds of rape, murder, robbery, and other crimes committed against the Mormons. When the Prophet Joseph could bear it no more, he rose to his feet and spoke with a voice of thunder: "Silence, ye fiends of the infernal pit. In the name of Jesus Christ I rebuke you, and command you to be still; I will not live another minute and hear such language. Cease such talk, or you or I die this instant!"

Wrote Elder Pratt: "I have seen the ministers of justice, clothed in magisterial robes . . . in the Courts of England; I have witnessed a Congress in solemn session . . .; I have tried to conceive of kings . . .; and of emperors assembled to decide the fate of kingdoms; but dignity and majesty have I seen but once, as it stood in chains, at midnight, in a dungeon in an obscure village of Missouri."[20]

There was a man! Joseph Smith, the prophet of the Restoration.

The Savior, the perfect model of manliness, stood before his tormentors, having been scourged, beaten, spat upon, and crowned with platted thorns. Pilate admitted, "I find no fault in him." Then he pronounced those irrefutable and piercing words: "Behold the man!"[21]

Jesus, our Savior, was *the* man among men, for he "increased in wisdom and stature, and in favour with God and man;"[22] he subjected the flesh to the Spirit and yielded not to temptation;[23] he learned obedience by the things which he suffered;[24] he grew from grace to grace.[25]

Thus he, the only sinless and perfect man who ever walked this earth, is qualified to state: "What manner of men ought ye to be? Verily I say unto you, even as I am."[26]

King David instructed his son Solomon: "Be thou strong . . . and shew thyself a man; and keep the charge of the Lord thy God to walk in his ways, to keep his statutes, and his commandments . . . that thou mayest prosper in all that thou doest."[27] I echo this charge to the young men of the Church. Be men! Be men of Christ! Be men of God!

Notes

1. John W. Santrock, *Life-Span Development* (Dubuque, Iowa: William C. Brown, Co., 1983), p. 404.

2. Carlos E. Asay, *In the Lord's Service*, p. 46.

3. Jacob 2:7.

4. See 1 Corinthians 14:8–11.

5. Genesis 1:27; see also Alma 5:14, 19.

6. Psalm 8:4–5.

7. See 1 Peter 2:9; Acts 17:28; Hebrews 12:9.

8. See 1 Corinthians 3:16–17.

9. 2 Nephi 1:21.

10. 2 Nephi 1:13.

11. 2 Nephi 1:21.

12. 2 Nephi 1:23–24.

13. See 2 Nephi 26:22; Alma 5:7.

14. See Ephesians 6:11–18.

15. See D&C 103:9–10.

16. See James 1:8.

17. A. Conan Doyle, *The White Company*, pp. 58–59.

18. 2 Nephi 9:39.

19. See Ezra Taft Benson, *Cross Fire: The Eight Years with Eisenhower* (Garden City, N.Y.: Doubleday, 1962), pp. 486–87.

20. *Autobiography of Parley P. Pratt* (Salt Lake City: Deseret Book Co., 1961), p. 211.

21. Matthew 27:29; John 19:4–5.

22. Luke 2:52.

23. See Mosiah 15:1–8.

24. See Hebrews 5:8.

25. See D&C 93:12–14.

26. 3 Nephi 27:27.

27. 1 Kings 2:2–3.

CHAPTER 9

An Invitation to Young Men and Women
Yield to the Enticings
of the Holy Spirit

*L*inda was a very popular seventeen-year-old who loved the noise of the crowd. She seemed happiest when involved in activities where people mingled freely and engaged in boisterous conversation. No one was surprised when she was chosen as a school cheerleader. After all, she could jump and shout and stir excitement among a group of people as well as anyone.

Slowly, but progressively, the voices of the peer group gained control of Linda's life, for she wanted to be acceptable to everyone, particularly to those who seemed to be the most sophisticated and "fun" oriented. In time the enticements of her carnally minded friends became more appealing than the warnings of her caring parents. Worse still, the numbing effects of tobacco, alcohol, and other addictive substances little by little smothered the voice of conscience. Before long, Linda yielded completely to the voices of the world—voices that had convinced her that happiness could be gained by forsaking parental restraints, rules of society, and other quieting influences in her life.

At the urgings of a lustful companion, Linda ran away from home. They were not concerned about marriage or other conventional arrangements. It was the "good time" that the two sought. Thoughts of basking under the lights of the big city and blending their voices with others who were rebelling against heaven and home seemed to push them on their way.

Once in the city, the young couple chased their dismal dream. It was one binge after another and one nightclub after another, with all the assorted baggage attached. Soon, however, the dream turned into a nightmare. Their funds were exhausted. Too proud and ashamed to return home, they looked for jobs and some means of sustaining their style of living in the so-called "fast lane." But it wasn't easy for two high school dropouts to find employment. Neither possessed a marketable skill, and what friends they had made during the short and carefree days pushed them aside.

As their circumstances became more desperate, Linda and her companion began to blame each other for what had happened. Eventually they decided to go it alone, because the stresses of adversity had destroyed all that remained of their pseudo-love.

Linda moved from one job to another—one economic crisis to another. First, it was washing dishes in a dirty café. Next, it was sweeping the floor in a smelly saloon. Each task was more demeaning than the last and each took its toll on her ego and self-esteem. Finally, in sheer desperation, Linda turned to prostitution.

A year passed, but it seemed like an eternity to Linda. Her life was one one-night stand after another with a parade of nameless individuals who treated her like a rented tool. She became zombie-like, hardly heeding the meaningless voices around her and the bright lights of the big city—lights that had drawn her away from home and burned her like an innocent moth. Life, she finally concluded, was not worth living.

One evening, Linda decided that things must change. She crawled out of bed without awakening her bed partner, dressed, and walked the noisy streets of the city. She wondered what she might do to escape her dreary and empty existence.

In the midst of Linda's aimless wandering, thoughts of

home flooded through her mind. She remembered the warmth and beauty of the place where Mother and Father showered her with love. She recalled many fond memories associated with brothers, sisters, and other members of the family circle. Moreover, she brooded over the feelings of peace and security that had once been hers when living within the quiet company of people who had extended unselfish love to her. Her heart yearned for home and the voice within cried, "Go there!"

But she had concerns. She wondered whether those at home would accept her after all the mistakes she had made. Will they forgive me? was the question that repeated itself over and over again in her mind.

Then she remembered a lesson her father had taught the family about the forgiveness of sins after repentance and through the merits of Christ. Moreover, she recalled her father reading and discussing the parable of the prodigal son—a tender story that had caused her and other listeners to weep openly.

Linda thought to herself: I am the prodigal; I did rebel; I have erred; and I have eaten with the swine. So I must go home and trust that they will receive me.

She had barely enough money to buy a one-way bus ticket home; yet she bought it, knowing of no other way to climb out of the pit she had dug for herself. It was a long ride back to the little town where she had grown up. The miles seemed to drag by. En route she replayed the twelve-month nightmare over and over again in her mind. How foolish she had been! Why had she listened to the enticing voices of the world? With each thought came regrets and bitter tears.

The walk from the bus station to home seemed long and arduous. Part of Linda's body wanted to run. Another part held back because of the uncertainties of the reception. One voice within her shouted, "Turn back, they don't want to see you ever again." A still, small voice whispered, "They love you and they want you to come back home."

She hesitated in front of the house. But as she reached to open the front gate to the yard, the door of the house flew open and out streamed the whole family. All members of the family cradled her in their arms and smothered her with kisses, for this their daughter and sister "was dead and is alive again; and was lost, and is found."[1]

Later in the day Linda learned of the power that turned her homeward. She was informed that family and friends had gathered on that weekend fasting and praying that she would be found and returned safely to their care. The loud and barbaric voices of Blindness of Mind and Hardness of Heart had lured her away from loved ones. Soft and kind voices—even the enticings of the Holy Spirit—had brought her back.

It is important that you keep in mind the miracle of forgiveness through the goodness and grace of our Savior. Many rejoice when the sinner comes to himself and repents. But it is also very important that you remember this unchanging truth: "That man [or woman] who resists temptation and lives without sin is far better off than the man [or woman] who has fallen, no matter how repentant the latter may be. . . . How much better it is never to have committed the sin!"[2]

Many Kinds of Voices

Have you ever stopped to count the number of voices you hear each day? If you have, you know that there is a chorus of people calling out for your attention. There are the voices at home, in school, over the radio, through the television set, on the street, at work, and everywhere you go. Some of these voices are friendly and have your best interests at heart. Others are not so friendly and belong to people whose love for you is only as deep as your pocketbook. Nonetheless, all of these friendly and unfriendly voices can influence your thoughts and actions for better or for worse, whether you are aware of it or not. As one inspired man put it, "There are . . . so many kinds of voices in the world, and none of them is without signification."[3]

Many of the voices you hear convey very enticing messages, such as "Come here," "Buy this," "Do this," "Do that." These are only a few of the sounds that bombard your ears each day. Not all of these voices and messages are evil; but some are seductive invitations issued by men and women with bad intent. As messages are communicated verbally, visually, or in print, you must sift carefully the good from the bad. Otherwise you may be enticed to travel down strange roads toward bright lights and wrong destinations, just as Linda and her companion were led.

Voices of Good and Bad Spirits

In addition to the many kinds of voices in the world already mentioned, there are other less audible voices of great significance. One prophet made reference to the voice of a good spirit and the voice of an evil spirit by saying that people "reap eternal happiness or eternal misery, according to the spirit which they listed to obey, whether it be a good spirit or a bad one. For every man receiveth wages of him whom he listeth to obey."[4]

Obviously, the good spirit is the Spirit of the Lord. The evil spirit is that of Satan, who rebelled against God from the very beginning, swearing that he would make you and others "miserable like unto himself."[5] Both spirits are real. Depending on how individuals respond to their voices, one has the power to bless the lives of all members of the human family; the other, the power to curse them all. Both are significant voices!

You might wonder why a loving Heavenly Father would subject you to a war of words and feelings. "If he loved me," you may say, "why would he allow Satan and his cheerleaders to confuse me with words or impressions that can hurt me?" You may be assured that God is not playing a game with you. He loves you and he wants you to grow and to become like him. Therefore he has placed you in the school of mortality, where there is an opposition in all things, along with moral agency; where choices must be made, and where you and all others will be put to the test. God's own words are: "We will make an earth whereon these [God's children] may dwell; and we will prove them herewith, to see if they will do all things whatsoever the Lord their God shall command them."[6]

The Spirit of Christ

In His infinite wisdom and grace, the Lord has provided you with a means of discerning the goodness and badness of messages spoken to you while attending the school of mortality. That means of discernment is known as the Spirit of Christ—a spirit given to every child who is born into this world. For those who will heed it, this spirit "inviteth and enticeth to do good continually." It also provides a way whereby the merits of something may be assessed. Whenever you are called upon to judge the worthiness of any voice or any prompting, remember this: everything that prompts you to pray, everything that entices you to do good, and everything that persuades you to believe in Christ, "is sent forth by the power and gift of Christ; wherefore ye may know with a perfect knowledge it is of God."[7]

So I admonish you to "search diligently in the light [or Spirit] of Christ that ye may know good from evil; and . . . lay hold upon every good thing."[8]

Elder Joseph F. Merrill made a simple comparison of the two spirits competing for your attention: "The Spirit of the Lord is comforting, joy-producing, love-inspiring, help-giving. The spirit of the devil is manifested in fault-finding, envy, selfishness, hatred, deceit, dishonesty, and produces misery, sin and crime."[9]

Conscience

A related power given you whereby enticing voices may be judged is conscience. President Marion G. Romney explained that the Spirit of Christ "is, no doubt, the source of one's conscience, which Webster defines as 'a knowledge or feeling of right and wrong, with a compulsion to do right' . . ."[10] President Joseph F. Smith stated that the Spirit of Christ "quickens the conscience of man and gives him intelligence to judge between good and evil, light and darkness, right and wrong."[11] Elder Bruce R. McConkie wrote that conscience "is an inborn consciousness or sense of the moral goodness or blameworthiness of one's conduct, intentions, and character, together with an instinctive feeling or obligation to do right or be good."[12]

You need not worry about whether the Spirit of Christ is the source of one's conscience or whether the Spirit of Christ quickens the conscience. What you should understand, however, is that conscience is a spiritual monitor or type of personal director or compass, so long as you use it properly. Much like the Liahona,[13] conscience will guide you down wisdom's path so long as you exercise faith, live righteously, and yield to the enticings of the Holy Spirit.

Battles of the Soul

You are a rare exception, indeed, if you have never experienced a battle within your own soul, wherein conscience was pitted against the tempter's alluring voice. You know how the war was waged. The one voice whispered: "Go ahead, do it; no one is watching; you know it's wrong, but you can repent tomorrow; you'll do it only this time; you are only hurting yourself, but the thrill of doing it far outweighs the fleeting pain involved"; and so on.

Then, the other voice spoke: "You know it is wrong; it is contrary to all you have been taught; you and those who love you will be offended; it will weaken your resolve and ability to resist in the face of other temptations; it will leave a bad taste in your mouth, and it will scar your character; it will drive away the Holy Spirit"; and so on.

If you yield to the enticings of the tempter or evil spirit you will be required to suffer the consequences, including the pains of regret, remorse, a scarred conscience, and loss of spirituality. On the other hand, if you yield to the enticings of the good spirit or the conscience, you will enjoy peace of mind, joy, an increase in personal goodness, and many other blessings. Don't forget that the conscience is a very delicate portion of your being. It is a spiritual instrument that can be desensitized through wanton sinning and gross neglect. It can also be more keenly attuned through personal righteousness. Ignore it or offend it long enough and it becomes numbed and is rendered useless. Use it and yield to its counsel consistently and the voice becomes more and more distinct. Case in point: Nephi prospered because he obeyed the good spirit. He heard, he felt, and he obeyed. Laman and Lemuel, however, rebelled against the promptings of the still, small voice to the extent that they were past feeling and could not feel his words.[14]

"Let No Man Despise Thy Youth"

I like the timeless counsel the Apostle Paul gave to a young believer by the name of Timothy. Said he, "Let no man despise thy youth; but be thou an example of the believers, in word, in conversation, in charity, in spirit, in faith, in purity."[15] Just exactly what Paul had in mind when these words were written, I don't know. But this I do know: young people have been, are now, and always will be threatened by those who would steal their time, health, virtue, and even faith.

Today the dealers of pornography, sex, alcohol, tobacco, narcotics, and other forms of vice hate the souls of youth but love their money and resources. Such despisers of youth would make slaves of the young by drowning them in the addictive works of the flesh.[16] So they raise their voices high and seek to entice young people to get lost down strange roads with dead ends. Their contempt for you is evidenced in the trail of broken hearts, broken promises, and broken health (physical and spiritual) they leave behind.

On one occasion, Jesus warned, "Take heed that ye despise not one of these little ones . . . ; (for) whoso shall offend one of these little ones which believe in me, it were better for him that a millstone were hanged about his neck, and that he were drowned in the depth of the sea."[17]

These are strong words spoken against those who would injure innocent children. I wonder, however, how the Lord feels about those who injure youth. Surely their crime is not much less than those who offend children. Maybe the offenders of youth will not feel the weight of millstones about their necks; yet I feel confident that they will suffer serious consequences for deceiving, defiling, delaying, and demeaning youth.

"Neglect Not the Gift"

After warning him against those who might despise his youth, the Apostle Paul counselled Timothy, "Neglect not the gift that is in thee, which was given thee by prophecy, with the laying on of the hands of the presbytery. Meditate upon these things; give thyself wholly to them; that thy profiting may appear to all. Take heed unto thyself, and unto the doctrine; continue in them: for in doing this thou shalt both save thyself, and them that hear thee."[18]

Timothy, like you and all other young people, had been blessed with the Light of Christ and a conscience. But Timothy possessed something more. He had been baptized and had been given the Holy Ghost by the laying on of hands. With other true believers, he was made a partaker of the "heavenly gift."[19]

Much has been preached and written about the Holy Ghost. You will want to learn all you can about him and his powers. For now, however, ponder President Kimball's summary of the gift that you must not neglect:

> The Holy Ghost is a revelator. Every worthy soul is entitled to a revelation, and it comes through the Holy Ghost. In Moroni's farewell to the Lamanites, he says: "And by the power of the Holy Ghost ye may know the truth of all things" (Moroni 10:5).
>
> He is a reminder and will bring to our remembrance the things which we have learned and which we need in the time thereof. He is an inspirer and will put words in our mouths, enlighten our understandings and direct our thoughts. He is a testifier and will bear record to us of the divinity of the Father and the Son and of their mission and of the program which they have given us. He is a teacher and will increase our knowledge. He is a companion and will walk with us, inspiring us all along the way, guiding our footsteps, impeaching our weaknesses, strengthening our resolves, and revealing to us righteous aims and purposes.[20]

Those who despise youth would have you believe that the Holy Ghost is a thing of the past. They admit that this power was received and enjoyed by people in ancient times, but at the same time they deny the need for such a gift in our modern day. Unfortunately they are not familiar with this declared testimony: "The Holy Ghost . . . is the gift of God unto all those who diligently seek him, as well in times of old as in the time that he should manifest himself unto the children of men. . . . For he that diligently seeketh shall find; and the mysteries of God shall be unfolded unto them, by the power of the Holy Ghost, as well in these times as in times of old, and as well in times of old as in times to come."[21]

Temples of God

The Apostle Paul pleaded with Timothy to take heed unto himself and the doctrine, because he knew that the Holy Spirit will not remain in the presence of unclean people. Paul had taught another group of Church members: "Know ye not that your body is the temple of the Holy Ghost which is in you." "If any man defile the temple of God, him shall God destroy; for the temple of God is holy, which temple ye are."[22]

You must understand that "no unclean thing can dwell with God."[23] Similarly, "[God] doth not dwell in unholy temples."[24] Therefore, "let virtue garnish thy thoughts unceasingly," "speak with the tongue of angels," and "be . . . doers of the word, and not hearers only." Then the Holy Ghost, the unspeakable gift, will be your constant companion.[25]

Do you want to live an almost errorless life? Would you like to have experiences wherein you perform beyond your natural abilities? How would you like to receive personal inspiration from heaven? Have you ever heard the whisperings of the still, small voice within you? When was the last time you had new thoughts planted in your mind? These and other marvelous experiences can be yours if you yield to the enticings of the Holy Spirit.

A few young people do walk the slippery path of youth

without stumbling or falling somewhere along the way. They do so because they court the Holy Spirit, obey God and parents, and do all else necessary to avoid Hardness of Heart and Blindness of Mind. More than a few, however, run into problems and suffer serious setbacks at one time or another.

Earlier in this chapter, I told about Linda and her rebellious companion. They are representative of all young men and women who listen to the wrong voices and who therefore suffer bitter consequences. However, Linda is also representative of those who trust in God and repent, thus casting their burdens upon the Savior of mankind. No, repentance is not easy, nor is it without pain. (How much better it is to avoid the mistake or transgression altogether!) But when it is required, you must look to God with faith and present a broken heart and a contrite spirit so that you can experience the miracle of forgiveness.

On the Road to Nowhere

When I first learned about Morris, he was in prison. He had grown up with crime. Both his father and his mother were convicts and alcoholics. He had been on his own since he was six years old. When he was thirteen, the flu epidemic took all the members of his family in death. After the funerals, Morris hopped on a freight train and began a nomadic life across the nation. This life included crime, which began with car theft and then extended to burglaries and armed robberies.

After spending several years in prison, Morris realized it was a dead-end existence. He came to the realization that he was going further and further on the road to nowhere. In his own words he wrote: "I slowly came to realize I did not like myself. How could I change? If I kept up my criminal acts, I would die in a prison cell and be buried in some unmarked plot on prison property. I did not know anything about religion. I began to read and investigate various religions with an open mind, seeking insight, looking for a commitment, for the first time in my life, that was positive in nature."

Slowly and progressively Morris gained a knowledge of the gospel and gained a testimony of Jesus Christ. This newfound knowledge and testimony enabled him to overcome his bad habits and to change his behavior completely. His approach was to learn a principle of truth, then live it as perfectly as possible. Principle by principle he climbed out of his pit of sin and emerged as a man of faith and righteousness.

Morris's Lamb Story

Morris's story was much like Linda's, only worse. He too listened to the wrong voices and made gross mistakes. Nonetheless, he came to himself in time and cleaned up his life. After his rather painful lesson, he wrote in a letter: "There is a story that a number of years ago a lighthouse was being constructed on the coast of Wales. When it was nearly completed, one of the laborers stumbled and fell from the scaffold to the rocks below. Very sad, the other workmen backed down the ladder to tend to the broken body of their friend. To their great surprise and much joy, they saw him lying, shaken and bruised, but not severely harmed. Beside him lay a dead lamb. A flock of sheep had been feeding below the structure and a lamb had broken his fall."

Then, as a postscript, Morris added: "A lamb broke my fall, the Lamb of God. He that taketh away all the sins of the world. I may be bruised and bent, but I am on the way to recovery and I owe it all to the Lamb of God."

King Benjamin says it all in one profound verse of scripture: "For the natural man is an enemy to God, and has been from the fall of Adam, and will be, forever and ever, unless he yields to the enticings of the Holy Spirit, and putteth off the natural man and becometh a saint through the atonement of Christ the Lord, and becometh as a child, submissive, meek, humble, patient, full of love, willing to submit to all things which the Lord seeth fit to inflict upon him, even as a child doth submit to his father."[26]

*   *   *

Please be selective about the voices you listen to. Don't be confused or misled by the loud and seductive voices of the world. Rather, attune yourself to the voice of the Spirit and allow it to entice you toward good works and righteous living.

Notes

1. Luke 15:32.
2. Spencer W. Kimball, *The Miracle of Forgiveness*, p. 357.
3. 1 Corinthians 14:10.
4. Alma 3:26–27.
5. 2 Nephi 2:27.
6. Abraham 3:24–25.
7. Moroni 7:13–17.
8. Moroni 7:19–20.
9. Joseph F. Merrill, Conference Report, April 1941, p. 51.
10. Marion G. Romney, Conference Report, April 1977, pp. 59–61.
11. Joseph F. Smith, *Improvement Era*, March 1908, p. 380.
12. Bruce R. McConkie, *Mormon Doctrine*, 2nd ed. (Salt Lake City: Bookcraft, 1966), pp. 156–57.
13. See Alma 37:38.
14. See 1 Nephi 17:45.
15. 1 Timothy 4:12.
16. See Galatians 5:19–20.
17. Matthew 18:6; see also 18:10.
18. 1 Timothy 4:14–16.
19. 4 Nephi 1:3.
20. *The Teachings of Spencer W. Kimball*, p. 23.
21. 1 Nephi 10:17, 19.
22. 1 Corinthians 6:19; 3:17.
23. 1 Nephi 10:21.
24. Alma 7:21.
25. See D&C 121:45–46; 2 Nephi 32:2; James 1:22.
26. Mosiah 3:19.

Conclusion
Youth of the Noble Birthright

A. Conan Doyle wrote: "It is easy to sit in the sunshine and preach to the man [or woman] in the shadows."[1] Stated in another way, it is easy to act as a Saturday morning quarterback and replay the game lost the night before. All of us seem to have better hindsight (the ability to see after the event what should have been done) than foresight (the power to foresee and provide for the future). It is therefore easy for me to sit in the light shed by age and preach to those who are walking in the shadows or unknowns of youth.

I do not share my counsel and advice because I believe that I have made all the right choices during my life, or that I have all the right answers to the problems facing young people. I have made mistakes. Further, there are many things relating to the slippery path of youth that I do not understand fully. But I do possess a genuine love for youth and I have enjoyed a wealth of experience that I feel would be wasted if it were not passed like a baton into the hands of others. After all, if we of the fading generation lock up the virtue within us as though it

133

were some savage creature, what will happen to those of the rising generation?

Goodness of Youth

A young lady who was invited to read and critique a preliminary draft of this book is reported to have asked, "Why doesn't the author say something good about us?" This comment shocked me, to say the least. My intent has not been to be negative in any way. And if the stories used to illustrate my points of view come across as anti- this or anti- that, I apologize.

There are few who respect young men and women more than I. I know of their almost limitless energies and abilities, and I know of the many marvelous things they can accomplish when they keep youth, strength, and a clean life on their side.

I sing with fervor and deep feelings this line of a favorite hymn: "O youth of the noble birthright, Carry on, carry on, carry on!"[2]

Noble Birthright

I too believe that today's Latter-day Saint youth are blessed with a noble birthright, and I urge them to be wise enough to recognize it and strong enough to claim it. I do not refer to a birthright of lands and powers and privileges such as were extended to the firstborn in wealthy families of long ago. Rather, I speak of the unparalled opportunities for growth extended to young people of today who bask in "the times of restitution of all things, which God hath spoken by the mouth of all his holy prophets since the world began."[3]

In the Latter-day Saint context birthrights are not restricted to the firstborn or to just a few privileged individuals. They are extended to all who live as they should and who defend themselves against sin and ignorance. Said President Gordon B. Hinckley with prophetic insight: "My dear young [people], the Lord has been very good to you. He has brought you forth in this, the greatest age in the history of the earth. He has made you the beneficiary of His glorious gospel, restored to the earth for your blessing. No other generation has been the beneficiary of so much knowledge, of so much experience, of so much affluence and opportunity. . . . God bless you . . . you of the noble birthright, you of the great promise."[4]

There are great promises—even a noble birthright—offered without money and without price to those who live purposeful and righteous lives. Such promises, however, will not be served automatically on a silver platter to young people or claimed by default. Faith must be exercised and good works evidenced by all who want to claim the promises of a noble birthright. This fact is stated clearly in these words: "I, the Lord, am bound when ye do what I say; but when ye do not what I say, ye have no promise."[5]

Two Warnings

Two warnings, like golden threads, have been woven throughout the fabric of this book. Over and over again I have cautioned readers to avoid Blindness of Mind and Hardness of Heart. I have done this because the negative conditions personified by these names are the robbers, highwaymen, thugs, and pickpockets who deprive young people of their birthright of happiness through noble achievement.

I have, therefore, advised readers that Blindness of Mind is repelled by your—

- Setting worthy goals and striving to reach them.
- Cultivating personal gifts and talents and sharing them with others.
- Selecting righteous role models and following their example.

I have proposed that Hardness of Heart is overcome and rendered useless by your—

- Obeying God's commandments,
- Obeying loving parents, and
- Obeying the eternal rhythm of life.

At the same time I have counselled readers, especially those who are walking the slippery path of youth, to pay close attention to three road signs posted along the way. One is the warning: "Be cautious and do not confuse lust with love." Another is a charge: "Be men and women of God." The third is an invitation: "Yield to the enticings of the Holy Ghost."

These actions and related wholesome actions, if woven into the fabric of your lives, will stir "exceeding faith," promote "good works," and put to flight the enemies of your souls. Moreover, these golden thread actions cited above will invite into your presence the Spirit of the Lord—a power that enables you to perform beyond your natural abilities and realize seemingly impossible dreams.

Carry On

Said President Ezra Taft Benson to a gathering of youth:

> For nearly six thousand years God has held you in reserve to make your appearance in the final days before the Second Coming. Every previous gospel dispensation has drifted into apostasy, but ours will not. . . . God has saved for the final inning some of his strongest children, who will help bear off the kingdom triumphantly. And that is where you come in, for you are the generation that must be prepared to meet your God. . . . Make no mistake about it—you are a marked generation. There has never been more expected of the faithful in such a short period of time as there is of us. . . . Each day we personally make many decisions that show where our support will go. The final outcome is certain—the forces of righteousness will finally win. What remains to be seen is where each of us personally, now and in the future, will stand in this fight—and how tall we will stand. Will we be true to our last-days, foreordained mission?[6]

Each of you must answer President Benson's question in your own way. Each of you must decide whether you will sell, squander, or make the most of the next ten years of your life. I pray that you will make the right choices so that, in the end, you will have done and become all that you have dreamed about.

Notes

1. *The White Company*, p. 239.
2. "Carry On," *Hymns*, No. 255.
3. Acts 3:21.
4. Gordon B. Hinckley, *Ensign*, May 1987, p. 48.
5. D&C 82:10.
6. Quoted by Marvin J. Ashton, *Ensign*, November 1989, p. 36.

Epilogue
Would You Sell?

*E*arlier in this book I shared with you a beet field conversation with my stake president of some years ago. You will recall
that I rejected his offer of a hundred thousand dollars in exchange for ten years of my life. Among other things, I said to my
leader when the supposed proposition was made, "I would not
sell to you or anyone else. I have things to do in the years ahead
and I will not sell a part of my life for any amount of money."[1]

My years between eighteen and twenty-eight came and
went like "a vapour that appeareth for a little time, and then
vanisheth away."[2] I would be lying if I didn't admit that there
were times when the days seemed to drag on painfully slowly.
Yet looking back in perspective upon that decade of living, I see
it as an exciting and fulfilling time of varied and wonderful experiences—experiences that were refining in nature.

Have you any idea what I would have lost had I been willing and able to sell those years? Note this recap of what happened to me between age eighteen and age twenty-eight:

- I spent two years in the United States Army during World
  War II. This stint of military service was a precious time

of testing for me. I was exposed to people of different backgrounds and faiths. I was privileged to stand up for my own ideals, even to the point of defending my chosen way of living.

- I served more than two and a half years in the Palestine-Syrian Mission as a full-time missionary for The Church of Jesus Christ of Latter-day Saints. This experience was of eternal worth to me. Not only did I see an interesting part of the world that was full of historical and biblical significance but also I lived with people whose culture was different from mine and shared with them the best I had to offer—my testimony and selfless services.
- I studied four years at the University of Utah and participated in intercollegiate athletics. In many respects this too was a dream come true, for I had planned all my life to attend a university. Such experience enabled me to learn valuable things and meet some interesting people who pointed me toward a chosen profession.
- I taught one and a half years in the public schools. During this time my natural gifts came to the fore and personal interests seemed to reach a peak. Moreover, I discovered that teaching young people was more than the acquisition of a few skills; it was an art—the Master's art—that brought with it personal fulfillment found in few fields of labor.

Cradled within all of the experiences mentioned above was marriage in the temple to my childhood sweetheart and the births of a daughter and two sons.

Could one place a monetary value upon these formative years and experiences? Obviously, they are priceless. Each experience, in its own due time, helped to mold my character and polish my personality in one way or another. Each provided me with opportunities to grow and to become a better person. If I had lost or taken out of sequence even one of the grooming experiences associated with the years of eighteen to twenty-eight, I seriously wonder about the direction my life might have taken.

I now ask of you, my young friends, how much do the next

ten years mean to you? Though my time is running out and yours is only beginning, I will not offer to buy that which is yours and which is impossible for you to sell. I do, however, warn you in the spirit of helpfulness to guard against the wasting, squandering, and forfeiting of your precious privileges.

Your Next Ten Years

Just suppose that an angel of God appeared at your bedside tonight and announced that you had been selected by the Lord to perform some great work, such as:

- Being the parent,
- Raising a family,
- Fulfilling a mission for the Church,
- Working with people in a leadership position, or
- Performing humanitarian services requiring commitment and spiritual strength.

Would that kind of sobering experience with a heavenly messenger cause you to change your approach to the next ten years of your life?

I once asked a young lady that very question. Her response was: "No, it would not! I have already decided what I am going to do with my life, and if I prepare for the future properly, I'll be ready for whatever honor or responsibility comes my way."

This response pleased me very much, for the young lady's mind and heart were not centered upon winning the honors of the world or amassing a pile of earthly goods. She was obviously approaching the next ten years of her life with goals, a plan, a faith, and a deep commitment in place. It was her conviction that if she exercised faith and worked hard enough good things would result in her life, all in accord with divine will.

A few weeks after I spoke with this remarkable young lady, she wrote:

I turned eighteen last December. . . . The questions you asked me really made me look deep within myself and ponder if I am actually the best I can be. I am not—but have been on a steady uphill climb since that day.

Well, the next ten years of my life will definitely be busy and I know that I will have the opportunity to fulfill most of my temporal and spiritual goals. In three and a half years I will have finished university. I am studying for a double-degree in Arts and Commerce. I will also marry and begin a family—all within the Church."[3]

Not all youth are as mature or as well focused on the future as this young lady. Some may be sitting and waiting, hoping that something dramatic will occur, like the appearance of an angel. Such miracle seekers will probably be disappointed unless they change the direction of their lives.

It is true that the boy Samuel heard the voice of the Lord at night and went on to "do a [work] in Israel, at which both the ears of every one that heareth it [did] tingle."[4] It is true that an angel came to youthful Mary and informed her that she would give birth to the Son of God.[5] And it is also true that an angel appeared to a young man named Joseph Smith and informed him that "God had a work for [him] to do; and that [his] name should be had for good and evil among all nations, kindreds, and tongues . . ."[6] Normally, however, young people do not hear the voice of the Lord at night or receive angelic manifestations at the bedside wherein future events of their lives are forecast. Most young people are left with the private challenge of pursuing personal goals with faith in themselves, hope in the future, dependency upon the Lord, and the quiet whisperings of the Spirit to motivate them onward.

Build Your Defenses

I heard or read somewhere that one of our leaders expressed himself in words like these: "I have a greater sense of humility when addressing youth than in standing before kings and queens." One is humbled in the presence of young people because of who they are and who they may become. I too stand in awe of those of the rising generation who are firmly committed to the quest for success and happiness through the exercise of exceeding faith and involvement in good works.

You must, however, build your defenses, polish your armour, and resist the luring enticements of those highwaymen we have referred to as Blindness of Mind and Hardness of Heart.

Don't forget to pay close attention to the road signs posted along the slippery path of youth. These signs and related guideposts will ensure your safety and progress as you strive to accomplish significant things.

Go forward with staunch faith and firm resolve, courting the Spirit of God each and every day. Please, do not sell or squander the next ten years of your life! Make wise investment of your time, remembering that the days never show what the years will bring.

Notes

1. See Prologue.
2. James 4:14.
3. Part of a letter received from Samarica Payne of Victoria, Australia.
4. 1 Samuel 3:11.
5. Luke 1:26–36.
6. Joseph Smith—History 1:33.

Index